MW00396371

Annotated Teacher's Edition

WORLD OF VOCABULARY

TAN

Sidney J. Rauch

Alfred B. Weinstein

Assisted by Muriel Harris

Photo Credits

p. 2: Photofest; **p. 7:** Photofest; **p. 8:** Photofest; **p. 10:** Martha Swope; **p. 15:** Martha Swope; **p. 16:** Martha Swope; **p. 18:** © Jenny Hager. All rights reserved; **p. 23:** © Jenny Hager. All rights reserved; **p. 24:** © Jenny Hager. All rights reserved; **p. 26:** Office of the Governor, Commonwealth of Virginia; **p. 31:** Office of the Governor, Commonwealth of Virginia; **p. 32:** Mike Geissinger/NYT Pictures; **p. 34:** Wide World Photos; **p. 39:** © John V. Dunnigan/DPI; **p. 40:** Wide World Photos; **p. 42:** Wide World Photos; **p. 47:** Wide World Photos; **p. 48:** Wide World Photos; **p. 50:** © Karen Halverson/Omni-Photo Communications, Inc.; **p. 55:** © Howard Harrison Studio/DPI; **p. 56:** © Karen Halverson/Omni-Photo Communications, Inc.; **p. 58:** Courtesy of Harcourt Brace Javanovich; **p. 63:** Courtesy of Harcourt Brace Javanovich; **p. 64:** Courtesy of Harcourt Brace Javanovich; **p. 66:** UPI/The Bettmann Archive; **p. 71:** UPI/The Bettmann Archive; **p. 72:** UPI/The Bettmann Archive; **p. 74:** The Granger Collection; **p. 79:** The Granger Collection; **p. 80:** The Granger Collection; **p. 82:** Anthony Savignano/Galella, Ltd.; **p. 87:** Photofest; **p. 88:** Anthony Savignano/Galella, Ltd.; **p. 90:** Photofest; **p. 95:** Photofest; **p. 97:** Photofest; **p. 98:** Wide World Photos; **p. 103:** Photofest; **p. 104:** Wide World Photos; **p. 106:** Chris Helfin, Shooting Back; **p. 111:** Official White House Photo; **p. 112:** Davidica—Little Spotted Horse, Shooting Back; **p. 114:** © Jules Zalon/DPI; **p. 119:** © Linda Moser/DPI; **p. 120:** © Jules Zalon/DPI.

World of Vocabulary, Tan Level, Third Edition

Sidney J. Rauch • **Alfred B. Weinstein**

Copyright © 1996 by Globe Fearon Educational Publisher, a division of Paramount Publishing, One Lake Street, Upper Saddle River, New Jersey 07458. All rights reserved. No part of this book may be reproduced or transmitted in any form or by any means, electrical or mechanical, including photocopying, recording, or by any information storage and retrieval system without permission in writing from the publisher.

Printed in the United States of America

2 3 4 5 6 7 8 9 10   99 98

ISBN: 0-8359-1282-5

CONTENTS

>>>> *Program Overview*

The eight levels in the *World of Vocabulary* series are especially designed to interest ESL/LEP students and students who have been reluctant or slow to expand their vocabularies. As an effective alternative to traditional vocabulary development programs, each lesson in *World of Vocabulary* offers:

- a short, high-interest, nonfiction article that incorporates the key words for that lesson in a meaningful context.
- photographs that hold students' attention and provide additional context for the key words.
- a variety of short skills exercises that build understanding and retention.
- high-interest writing and simple research projects that offer opportunities for students to extend their learning.

This revised edition of *World of Vocabulary* includes new and updated lessons at all levels and a *Diagnostic and Placement Guide* to aid diagnosis and placement within the *World of Vocabulary* series. New stories in all eight levels spotlight personalities, such as Jim Carrey, Sandra Cisneros, and Steven Spielberg, and cover topics as engaging as World Cup soccer, Navajo code talkers, "Star Trek," and a group of Los Angeles teenagers who make and sell "Food from the 'Hood."

The revised series continues to offer diverse subjects and now includes selections on Latino actor Edward James Olmos, African American writer Walter Dean Myers, Native American ballerina Maria Tallchief, Latino baseball legend Roberto Clemente, Puerto Rican writer Nicholasa Mohr, and Chinese American writer Laurence Yep.

All eight levels continue to have color designations rather than numbers to prevent students from identifying the books with grade levels. The use of color levels also enables teachers to provide individual students with the appropriate reading skills and vocabulary enhancement without calling attention to their reading levels. Below are the revised *World of Vocabulary* levels listed by color and reading level:

Yellow	3
Tan	4
Aqua	5
Orange	6
Blue	7
Red	8
Purple	9
Green	10

As in the earlier version of *World of Vocabulary*, some lesson elements are carried throughout the series, but the pedagogy and design of each book is geared to the needs of students at that level. For example, the Yellow and Tan books are set in a larger typeface and have more write-on space for student responses than the other six books. Each lesson in these first two books contains eight key vocabulary words, compared to ten key words in the other books.

The Yellow and Tan books also include 15 units rather than the 20 units in the other books in the series. "Using Your Language" exercises in the Yellow and Tan books teach fundamental language skills that may need reinforcement at this reading level. The Tan book adds a phonics exercise.

As the reading level progresses in the next six books, the exercises offer more vocabulary words and increasing challenges. For example, "Find the Analogies" exercises appear in some lessons at the Aqua, Orange, and Red levels but are a part of every lesson in the Blue, Purple, and Green books.

>>>> The Need for Vocabulary Development

Learning depends on the comprehension and use of words. Students who learn new words and add them to their working vocabularies increase their chances for success in all subject areas.

Understanding new words is especially crucial for remedial and second-language learners. Their reluctance or inability to read makes it even more difficult for them to tackle unfamiliar words. The *World of Vocabulary* series was created for these students. The reading level of each selection is carefully controlled so students will not be burdened with an overload of new words.

Most importantly, the *World of Vocabulary* series motivates students by inviting them to relate their own experiences and ideas to the selections. In doing so, students gain essential practice in the interrelated skills of listening, speaking, reading, and writing. This practice and reinforcement enhances their vocabulary and language development.

>>>> Key Strategies Used in the Series

Providing Varied Experiences

The more varied experiences students have, the more meaning they can obtain from the printed word. For example, students who have studied the development of the space program will also have learned many new words, such as *astronaut* and *module*. They have also attached new meanings to old words, such as *shuttle* and *feedback*.

The reading selections in the *World of Vocabulary* series enable students to enrich their vocabulary by exploring major news events, as well as the lives and motivations of fascinating people. Through the wide range of selections, students encounter new words and learn different meanings of old words.

Visual tools are also valuable sources of experience. The full-page and smaller photographs in the lessons capture students' attention and help them to understand the words in the reading selections.

Building Motivation

If we can create the desire to read, we are on our way to successful teaching. Formal research and classroom experience have shown that the great majority of students are motivated to read if the following ingredients are present: opportunities for success, high-interest materials, appropriate reading levels, the chance to work at their own rate, and opportunities to share their experiences.

All of these ingredients are incorporated into the *World of Vocabulary* lessons through the use of engaging reading selections, controlled reading levels, a range of skills exercises, and discussion and enrichment opportunities.

Making Learning Meaningful

We do not often learn new words after one exposure, so vocabulary development requires repetition in meaningful situations. The *World of Vocabulary* series provides opportunities for students to use new words in relevant speaking and writing activities based on the high-interest reading selections.

Fostering Success

When students feel they have accomplished something, they want to continue. The *World of Vocabulary* series is designed to help students gain a feeling of accomplishment through listening, speaking, reading, and writing activities that motivate them to go beyond the lessons.

>>>> Readability Levels

The reading level in each lesson is controlled in two ways. First, vocabulary words appropriate to the designated reading level were selected from the EDL Core Vocabulary Cumulative List. The words were chosen for their interest, motivational level, and relevance to each reading selection.

Next, the reading level of each selection was adjusted using the Flesch-Kincaid Readability Index. This formula takes into account average sentence length, number of words per sentence, and number of syllables per word.

The new *Diagnostic and Placement Guide* provides an opportunity to diagnose students and place them into the appropriate levels of the series. The *Diagnostic and Placement Guide* offers tests that gauge students' vocabulary abilities and a scoring rubric to facilitate student placement.

VOCABULARY STRATEGIES

>>>> Learning and Thinking Styles

People of all ages learn and think in different ways. For example, most of us receive information through our five senses, but each of us tends to prefer learning through one sense, such as our visual or auditory modality.

By keeping in mind the different ways students learn and think, we can appeal to the range of learning and thinking styles. By taking different styles into account in planning lessons, we can help all students understand new information and ideas and apply this knowledge and insight to their lives.

There are three main learning styles:
- Visual learners like to see ideas.
- Auditory learners prefer to hear information.
- Kinesthetic or tactile learners absorb concepts better when they can move about and use their hands to feel and manipulate objects.

After we receive information, we tend to process or think about the information in one of two ways:
- Global thinkers prefer to see the "big picture," the whole idea or the general pattern, before they think about the details. They search for relationships among ideas and like to make generalizations. They are especially interested in material that relates to their own lives. Global thinkers tend to be impulsive and quick to respond to teachers' questions.
- Analytical thinkers focus first on the parts and then put them together to form a whole. They think in a step-by-step approach and look at information in a more impersonal way. They are more likely to analyze information and ideas rather than apply it to their own lives. Analytical thinkers tend to be reflective and thoughtful in their answers.

However, few of us are *only* auditory learners or *only* analytical thinkers. Most people use a combination of learning and thinking styles but prefer one modality or style over the others. An effective lesson takes into account all three types of learning and both types of thinking. The ideas below, in addition to your own creativity, will help you meet the needs and preferences of every student in your class.

Visual Learners
- Write the lesson's key vocabulary words on the chalkboard, overhead transparency, or poster so students can see the words and refer to them.
- Encourage students to examine the photographs in the lesson and to explain what the pictures tell them about the key words.
- Repeat oral instructions or write them on the board. After giving instructions, put examples on the board.

- Involve students in creating word cluster maps (see p. xiv) to help them analyze word meanings.
- Use the other graphic organizers on pp. xiii-xvii to help students put analogies and other ideas into a visual form.
- Display some of the writing assignments students complete for the "Learn More About..." sections. Encourage students to read each other's work.
- For selections that focus on authors or artists, collect books, pictures, or other works by that author or artist for students to examine.
- For selections that focus on actors, show videotapes of their movies or television shows.

Auditory Learners

- Invite a volunteer to read aloud the selection at the beginning of each unit as students follow along in their books. You might audiotape the selection so students can listen to it again on their own.
- Ask a student to read aloud the "Understanding the Story" questions.
- Provide time for class and small-group discussions.
- Read aloud the directions printed in the books.
- Occasionally do an activity orally as a class, such as "Complete the Story."
- Allow students to make oral presentations or to audiotape assignments from the "Learn More About..." sections.

Kinesthetic or Tactile Learners

- Encourage students to take notes so the movements of their hands can help them learn new information.
- Encourage students to draw pictures to illustrate new words.
- In small groups, have students act out new words as they say the words aloud.
- Invite students to clap out the syllable patterns and/or spellings of new words.

- Write (or have students write) the new words on cards that can be handled and distributed.
- Provide sets of letters that students can arrange to spell the key words.

Global Thinkers

- Explain the "big picture," or the general idea, first.
- Point out how the key words fit patterns students have studied and how they relate to words and concepts that are already familiar to students.
- Involve students in brainstorming and discussion groups. Encourage students to express ideas and images that they associate with the new words.
- Explore ways that ideas and information are relevant to students.
- Encourage students to think about their answers before they respond.
- Set goals and offer reinforcement for meeting those goals.

Analytical Thinkers

- Start with the facts and then offer an overview of the topic.
- Give students time to think about their answers before they respond.
- Encourage students to set their own goals and to provide their own reinforcement for meeting them.
- Suggest that students classify new words into several different categories.
- Provide time for students to organize concepts or processes in a step-by-step approach.
- Help students recognize how new concepts relate to their own lives.

>>>> Cooperative Learning

One way to address multiple learning and thinking styles and to engage students more actively in their own learning is through cooperative learning activities.

Cooperative learning means more than having students work in groups. They must work together toward a shared goal that depends on each person's contribution. In cooperative learning, group members share ideas and materials, divide task responsibilities among themselves, rely on each other to complete these responsibilities, and are rewarded as a group for successful completion of a task.

If your students are not accustomed to group work, you might assign (or have students choose) group roles, such as discussion leader, recorder, reporter, or timekeeper. Having specific responsibilities will help group members work together.

Cooperative learning has many applications in the *World of Vocabulary* series. For instance, you might organize the class into groups and have each group teach its own members the key vocabulary words in that lesson. Groups could use a jigsaw approach, with each person learning and then teaching two or three words to other members of the group. Groups might create their own word searches, flashcards, crossword puzzles, incomplete sentences, analogies, and so on.

Then evaluate each group member to determine his or her level of understanding. Or you might ask group members to number off so you can evaluate only the 3s, for example. Explain that you will hold the entire group accountable for those students' mastery of the lesson words.

In other applications of cooperative learning, students might work together to create one product, such as a cluster map, a simple research project, or an original story that incorporates the key vocabulary words.

You might also consider trying the cooperative learning activities below, modifying them so they will be appropriate for your students.

Word Round-Robin
Organize the class into groups of ten (eight for Yellow and Tan levels) and have each group sit in a circle. Ask members to count off 1-10 (or 1-8) and give everyone a sheet of paper. Assign all the 1s one vocabulary word from the lesson, the 2s another word, and so on. Then follow these steps:

Step 1: Ask students to write their assigned word and their best guess as to its definition.

Step 2: Have students pass their papers to the person on their right. Then tell them to read through the story to find the word on the paper they received. Have students write another definition below the first definition on the paper, using context clues from the story.

Step 3: Ask students to pass their papers to their right. This time tell students to use a dictionary to look up the word on the paper they received. Then have them write on the paper the dictionary definition and a sentence that includes the word, using the same meaning as in the story.

Step 4: Invite groups to read each paper aloud, discuss the word, and write one definition in their own words, based on what members wrote on the papers.

Step 5: Have each group share its definition for the assigned word with the class. Discuss similarities and differences among the definitions. Guide students to recognize that definitions of some new words are clear even in isolation because of their root words, while others have multiple definitions that depend on the context in which they are used.

Synonym Seekers
Involve the class in preparing for this activity by assigning a vocabulary word to each pair of students. (You might include words from more than one selection.) Each pair will write its word and as many synonyms as possible on an index card, consulting a dictionary and thesaurus, if you wish.

Have pairs share their cards with the class, explaining subtle differences among the synonyms. Then collect the cards and combine pairs of students to form teams of four or six. Call out one of the vocabulary words and ask teams to write down as many synonyms as they can think of in 30 seconds.

Then read the synonyms listed on the card. Teams will give themselves one point for each synonym they recalled. Encourage students to suggest new synonyms to add to the cards and discuss why certain words could not be used as synonyms. Play the game several times with these cards before creating new cards with other words.

>>>> Approaches for ESL/LEP Students

- Invite volunteers to read the stories aloud while students follow along in their books.
- Watch for figurative expressions in the lessons and discuss their literal and intended meanings. Examples include "making faces," "friendly fire," and "bounce off the walls."
- Help students identify root words. Involve them in listing other words with the same roots and in exploring their meanings.
- Compare how prefixes and suffixes in the vocabulary words are similar to those in words students already know.
- Make word webs to help students understand relationships among words and concepts. Use the graphic organizer on page xiv or write a vocabulary word in the center of the chalkboard or poster. Invite students to name as many related words as possible for you to write around the key word. Discuss how each word is related.
- Involve students in listing words that are similar in some way to a vocabulary word, such as other vehicles, adverbs, occupations, and so on.
- Encourage students to share words or phrases from their native languages that mean the same as the vocabulary words. Invite them to teach these

words from their native languages to the class.
- Arrange cooperative learning and other activities so ESL/LEP students are grouped with students who speak fluent English.
- Periodically group ESL/LEP students together so that they can assist one another in their native languages.
- Foster discussion with questions, such as "Do you think our space program should send more astronauts to the moon? Why?" and "Would you like to perform in a circus? Why?" These kinds of questions encourage students to use English to share their ideas and opinions.

>>>> Cross-Curricular Connections

General

- Challenge students to identify vocabulary words that have different meanings in other subject areas. For example, *fins* are defined as "rubber flippers" in the Aqua book. How are *fins* defined in science?
- Give extra credit to students who find the lesson's vocabulary words in other textbooks or in newspapers and magazines. Discuss whether the meaning is the same in both uses.

Math

- Invite pairs of students to write problems that include vocabulary words. The difficulty level will depend on their math skills. Ask pairs to exchange problems and try to solve each others'.

Language Arts

- Encourage students to write letters to some of the people described in the stories. Ask them to incorporate some of the lesson's key words into their letters.
- Have students, working in pairs or individually, write their own stories, using a certain number of vocabulary words from one or more selections.

They might leave the spaces blank and challenge other students to complete the stories correctly.

- Organize a spelling contest, using vocabulary words.
- Have groups prepare crossword puzzles that will be combined into a book.
- Encourage students to conduct surveys and/or interview people regarding topics that stem from the stories. For example, how many students or staff at school collect trading cards? What kinds do they collect? How many students or staff are "Star Trek" fans? What attracts them to "Star Trek"? Encourage students to graph their findings and to write short reports explaining their conclusions.

A SAMPLE LESSON PLAN

The following is a suggested plan for teaching a lesson from the *World of Vocabulary* series. You might use it as a guide for preparing and organizing your lessons. However, be sure to modify it where necessary to take into account your students' needs, abilities, interests, and learning styles, along with the specific exercises included in that lesson.

>>>> Setting Objectives

Each lesson in the *World of Vocabulary* series is based on the objectives below.

- To create enthusiasm for and an understanding of the importance of learning new words
- To improve reading comprehension by teaching the meanings of new words, stressing context clues
- To improve vocabulary by presenting key words in exercises that range from simple to complex and that allow for reinforcement of learning
- To encourage oral expression and motivate further study by introducing a highly interesting topic.

>>>> Stimulating Interest

Invite students to examine the photograph on the first page of the lesson. To stimulate their curiosity and involve them in the topic, ask questions. For example, if the lesson were about Koko the gorilla, you might ask:

- The gorilla in the picture is named Koko. How do you think Koko might be different from other gorillas?
- Do you think it is possible to teach a gorilla to talk? Why or why not?
- If Koko could talk to people, what do you think she might say?

>>>> Reading the Story

Have students read the story, silently or in small groups. You also might assign the story to be read outside class. To help auditory learners and ESL/LEP students, ask a volunteer to read the story aloud while classmates follow along in their books.

Encourage students to use the context clues in the story and the opening photograph to figure out the meanings of several boldfaced words. You might have students suggest a definition for each key word, based on context clues. Write the definitions on the chalkboard so the class can review and modify them later in the lesson.

As an aid to ESL/LEP students, discuss words or phrases in the story that have more than one meaning or that have figurative meanings. Two examples in the story about Koko are "blew kisses" and "spends some time."

>>>> Completing the Exercises

The information about exercises below is based on the lesson about Koko in the Orange level. However, books at different levels include different exercises. For example, the Yellow and Tan books offer a simpler activity called "Make a List" instead of the "Understanding the Story" exercise.

Students using the Yellow and Tan books also complete an exercise called "Find the Synonyms," while students at the Aqua, Orange, and Red levels have the "Complete the Sentences" exercise. The equivalent exercise for students at the Blue, Purple, and Green levels is called "Find the Analogies." Each level also includes a variety of other grammar and skills exercises.

Despite variations in exercises from level to level, the explanations below will help you understand why certain exercises are included and how they can be modified to support different learning and thinking styles.

>>>> "Understanding the Story"

This exercise usually asks students to determine the main idea of the selection and to make an inference as a way of assessing their general understanding of the story. Remember that global thinkers may have an easier time describing the main idea than analytical thinkers, who tend to focus on the parts of the story rather than the whole idea.

To use this as a cooperative activity, have students discuss the questions in groups of two or three. Then pair two groups so they can share their conclusions. Ask groups that disagreed on the answers to tell the class the reasoning for their different choices. Be sure to clear up any misunderstandings that become apparent without squelching creativity.

To make sure all students understand the general content of the story, ask a volunteer to summarize it in a sentence or two. Then give the analytical thinkers in the class an opportunity to contribute by describing some of the key supporting details in the story.

>>>> "Make an Alphabetical List"

This activity encourages students to study the key words closely and to become more familiar with their spellings. Practicing writing the words in alphabetical order will be especially beneficial for kinesthetic learners.

To check students' accuracy in arranging the words in alphabetical order, ask one or two students to read their lists aloud. Visual learners will appreciate seeing the list written on the board.

If necessary, model the pronunciation of certain words. Practice saying the more difficult words as a class. (This technique will also be helpful for ESL/LEP students.)

>>>> "What Do the Words Mean?"

In this exercise, students match the definitions listed in their books to the lesson's vocabulary words. If students offer other definitions for the same words, encourage them to consult a dictionary to check their accuracy. Many of the key words have different meanings in other contexts.

Encourage students to suggest synonyms for the words and perhaps some antonyms. Analytical learners might enjoy identifying root words and listing other words with the same roots, prefixes, or suffixes. Many ESL/LEP students will also benefit from this analysis.

>>>> "Complete the Sentences"

This exercise gives students another opportunity to practice using context clues as they complete a set of sentences using the key words.

>>>> "Use Your Own Words"

Working individually or in groups, students are encouraged to brainstorm words that describe a picture or express their reactions to it. This exercise fosters creativity involves students in the lesson by asking for their personal responses. Their responses will depend on their prior knowledge and individual perceptions, so answers are not included in the Answer Key. You might use some of the graphic organizers on pages xiii–xvii for this activity.

As a cooperative activity, students might enjoy working with three classmates to write a group description of the picture. Tell the first group member to write a word related to the picture on a sheet of paper and to pass the paper to the right. Have the next two group members add their own words, different from the ones already listed. Then ask the fourth group member to write one sentence about the picture that includes all three words. Start another sheet of paper with a different group member and continue in the same way, with the fourth member combining the words into one sentence.

>>>> "Make New Words from Old"

This is one of several reinforcement exercises throughout the *World of Vocabulary* series. "Make New Words from Old" invites students to look creatively at the letters in a key word from the lesson. Other exercises in the series challenge students to identify synonyms and/or antonyms, underline specific parts of speech, to find the subjects and predicates in sentences, to write the possessive forms of words, or to complete other activities that focus on key words from the lesson.

>>>> "Complete the Story"

Students again use context clues to place the lesson's key words correctly in a new story. This story relates to the one that opened the lesson and may offer more information on the topic or encourage students to apply new knowledge or insights in their own lives. You might use "Complete the Story" as a post-test of student mastery of the key words.

>>>> "Learn More About..."

The last page of each lesson offers one to four activities that encourage students to learn more about the lesson's topic. You might assign one or several activities or encourage students to choose an activity to complete for extra credit. They could work during class time or outside of class—individually, with partners, or in small groups.

Some of the activities are developed for ESL/LEP students, while others provide opportunities for cooperative learning, cross-curricular projects, and enrichment. Placing activities in these categories was not meant to limit their use, as many of the activities would benefit and interest most students. For some reluctant readers, these projects may be their first attempt at independent research, fueled by their interest in the lesson's topic.

Some lessons include a "Further Reading" activity that lists fiction or nonfiction books on the lesson's topic that are appropriate for that reading level. Students are asked to complete a brief activity after their reading.

"Further Reading" and other activities that require a written response provide additional opportunities for students to practice and receive feedback on their writing skills, including punctuation, capitalization, and spelling. The effort students spend on the "Learn More About" activities can result in marked improvements in their reading and writing skills.

UNDERSTANDING THE STORY

>>>> The topic of the story:

>>>> The main idea of the story:

>>>> Some details from the story:

>>>> What interested me most:

>>>> A question I would like to ask:

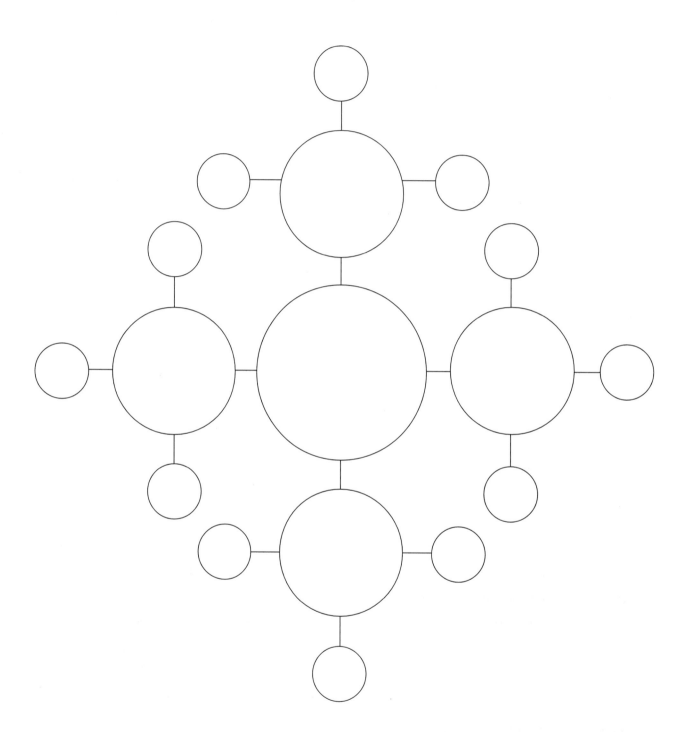

WORD CHART

A _____ is a _____ that
    (key word)   (description)

_____, _____, and
(characteristic)   (characteristic)

_____.
(characteristic)

ANALOGY ORGANIZER

relationship

_____ is to _____ [ ] as _____ is to _____.

relationship

_____ is to _____ [ ] as _____ is to _____.

relationship

_____ is to _____ [ ] as _____ is to _____.

relationship

_____ is to _____ [ ] as _____ is to _____.

relationship

_____ is to _____ [ ] as _____ is to _____.

USING THE GRAPHIC ORGANIZERS

Understanding the Story (page xiii)
This form will help students analyze the selection at the beginning of each unit and organize its content logically and visually.

Cluster Map (page xiv)
This organizer will help structure individual or group brainstorming sessions. Students write a key word or concept in the middle circle and related words or concepts in the adjoining circles.

Word Chart (page xv)
Students can use this chart to compare key words with similar words. They write words in the first column on the left and list categories across the top of the chart.

In another use of the chart, students might write adjectives in the left column. Across the top, they could list experiences.

Analogy Organizer (page xvi)
Students write in the box the relationship between the words in each pair. Then they write the three words given in the analogy in the blank spaces and choose a word listed in the book to complete the analogy. You might also use this graphic organizer to help students write their own analogies.

Venn Diagram (page xvii)
This organizer offers another way to compare the meanings of similar words. Students write the words to be compared above each circle. Then they list several properties that apply only to each word inside the circle and properties that the words share in the center area.

Tan Test Answers

1. responds
2. generation
3. exhibit
4. weary
5. construction
6. composer
7. shelters
8. major
9. examines; studies
10. cup; prize
11. fell; broke down
12. collecting; gathering
13. severe; very strong
14. mood; environment
15. enemies; rivals
16. combination; blend
17. Pavarotti; singer; voice
18. hotel; Detroit
19. movies; Edward James Olmos
20. dishes; China
21. stone; scientists; writing; Egypt
22. James; book
23. area; Mississippi River
24. father; engineer; Benton Electric Company
25. frustrated
26. experience
27. disability
28. exciting
29. limits
30. example
31. text
32. determination

TAN TEST

WHAT DO THE WORDS MEAN?

>>>> *Following are some meanings, or definitions, for the eight vocabulary words in the box below. Write the words next to their definitions.*

construction	weary	major	shelters
generation	exhibit	responds	composer

1. _____ answers; replies

2. _____ a period of time, about 30 years

3. _____ to place an object or objects on show

4. _____ tired; worn out

5. _____ the process of building

6. _____ a person who writes music

7. _____ places that give cover or protection

8. _____ important; principal

FIND THE SYNONYMS

>>>> A **synonym** is a word that means the same, or nearly the same, as another word. For example, *happy* and *glad* are synonyms.

>>>> *The column on the left contains eight vocabulary words. To the right of each word are three other words or groups of words. Two of these are synonyms for the vocabulary word. Circle the synonyms.*

9. **explores**	examines	affords	studies
10. **trophy**	cup	prize	winner
11. **collapsed**	objected	fell	broke down
12. **harvesting**	selecting	collecting	gathering
13. **intense**	severe	very strong	fragile
14. **atmosphere**	mood	program	environment
15. **opponents**	enemies	rivals	teammates
16. **mixture**	combination	juice	blend

USING YOUR LANGUAGE: Nouns

>>>> **Nouns** are words used to name people (*actor*), places (*city*), things (*cup*), actions (*objected*), and ideas (*legal*). Common nouns are names of any people, places, or things: *actor, city, cup*. Proper nouns are the names of particular people, places, or things: *Tom Cruise, Toledo, Grey Cup*.

Underline the nouns in each of the sentences below. Place one line under each common noun. Place two lines under each proper noun.

17. Pavarotti, the singer, has a beautiful voice.

18. We stayed in the biggest hotel in Detroit.

19. In which movies has Edward James Olmos appeared?

20. Those dishes are imported from China.

21. The Rosetta stone helped scientists understand ancient writing from Egypt.

22. James was intrigued by the book he was reading.

23. We lived in an area near the Mississippi River.

24. My father is an engineer for the Benton Electric Company.

COMPLETE THE STORY

>>>> *Use words from the box to fill in the blanks and complete the story. Use each word only once.*

disability	frustrated	exciting	limits
experience	determination	example	text

Shawn is a young mother who is losing her eyesight. Although she becomes (**25**) _____ at times when she bumps into furniture, she is treating this as a learning (**26**) _____. Shawn does not think of her problem as a (**27**) _____. Every day she comes up with (**28**) _____ new ideas for coping with the (**29**) _____ on her sight.

For (**30**) _____, Shawn is trying to get publishers to make the (**31**) _____ in picture books larger. That way, other mothers like her can still see the words and read to their children. Shawn may be losing her eyesight, but not her (**32**) _____ to live her life fully.

CONTENTS

1 SALSA STAR

Rubén Blades is a man of many **talents.** He is a **composer,** a singer, an actor, and even a lawyer. Blades writes and sings *salsa* songs. (The word *salsa* means "hot sauce" in Spanish.)

Most *salsa* songs are dance tunes. But Blades's songs tell important stories we do not usually hear about in songs. Blades sings about the evils of greed and laziness. Some of his songs are about his love of truth and **justice.**

Blades's acting career has added to his fame. He played a sheriff in the movie *The Milagro Beanfield War*. He **appeared** with Jack Nicholson in *The Two Jakes*. He acted with Joe Pesci in the film *The Super*.

Rubén Blades was born in Panama in 1948. He came to the United States in 1974. Now that he is famous, Blades is trying to **aid** the poor people of Panama. He wants to improve the living conditions of his people.

Although Rubén Blades is a Harvard-educated lawyer, he has not yet used his **legal** training. But Blades is thinking of a career in government. When people ask if he would ever run for the office of president of Panama, Blades **responds,** "Why not?" For this **singular** man, anything is possible.

MAKE A LIST

>>>> *There are eight vocabulary words in this lesson. In the story, they are boxed in color. Copy the vocabulary words here.*

1. talents
2. composer
3. justice
4. appeared
5. aid
6. legal
7. responds
8. singular

MAKE AN ALPHABETICAL LIST

>>>> *Here are the eight words you copied on the previous page. Write them in alphabetical order in the spaces below.*

| justice | legal | composer | responds |
| talents | aid | singular | appeared |

1. aid
2. appeared
3. composer
4. justice

5. legal
6. responds
7. singular
8. talents

WHAT DO THE WORDS MEAN?

>>>> *Following are some meanings, or definitions, for the eight vocabulary words in this lesson. Write the words next to their definitions.*

1. responds — answers; replies

2. appeared — was seen (on stage or screen); performed

3. composer — a person who writes music

4. legal — having to do with the law or with lawyers

5. aid — to help; to give what is useful or necessary

6. justice — fairness; rightfulness

7. singular — worthy of notice; remarkable

8. talents — special or natural abilities; skills

>>>> It is important to know the short vowel sounds. Remember: the vowels are *a, e, i, o, u,* and sometimes *y.*

Below are some words that contain the short vowel sounds. Look at them carefully and say them slowly. Stretch out the sounds so you can hear the vowels.

You will notice that when there is just one vowel sound in a word, it has the short vowel sound. A short vowel is marked by putting a small curved mark—for example, *ŭ*—above the letter.

>>>> Here are two samples of each of the short vowels.

short ă	short ĕ	short ĭ	short ŏ	short ŭ
măt	lĕt	fĭt	ŏx	ŭp
băttle	bĕd	fĭddle	bŏttle	ŭnder

>>>> *Underline each word in parentheses that has a short vowel sound. Then draw a ˘ above the short vowel.*

1. Susan left the (plate, dĭsh) on the table.
2. If you (shake, rŏck) the tree, the apples will fall.
3. We have a large (pile, stăck) of coins.
4. I don't know why he (yĕlls, screams) so much.
5. (Jane, Jăn) was the first one in line for tickets.
6. Our puppy plays (cute, fŭnny) tricks.

5

>>>> A **synonym** is a word that means the same, or nearly the same, as another word. *Happy* and *glad* are synonyms.

>>>> *The column on the left contains the eight key words in the story. To the right of each key word are three other words or groups of words. Two of these are synonyms for the key word. Circle the two synonyms.*

1. **aid** (to assist) to harm (to help)

2. **justice** (rightfulness) (fair play) conduct

3. **talents** (abilities) celebrations (skills)

4. **singular** (extraordinary) unnoticed (amazing)

5. **appeared** (performed) (came into view) vanished

6. **responds** asks (says) (replies)

7. **composer** (creator) (song writer) singer

8. **legal** (having to do with the law) having to do with eagles (having to do with lawyers)

>>>> *In each of the following sentences, there are words that need capital letters. Rewrite each sentence with the words correctly capitalized. Remember that capital letters are used in the following places: in the first word in a sentence; names of people, cars, cities, states, countries; days of the week; months of the year.*

1. when rubén blades came to the united states from panama, he was 26 years old.

   When Rubén Blades came to the United States from Panama, he was 26 years old.

2. rubén blades sang at the salsa festival, which was held at madison square garden in new york city.

   Rubén Blades sang at the Salsa Festival, which was held at Madison Square Garden in New York City.

3. he won his first grammy award for the album "escenas," which included a song with linda ronstadt.

   He won his first Grammy Award for the album "Escenas," which included a song with Linda Ronstadt.

USE YOUR OWN WORDS

>>>> *Look at the picture. What words come into your mind other than the ones you just matched with their synonyms? Write them on the lines below. To help you get started, here are two good words:*

1. _____smile_____   5. _____

2. _____mustache_____   6. _____

3. ___Answers will vary.___   7. _____

4. _____   8. _____

8

COMPLETE THE STORY

▶▶▶▶ Here are the eight vocabulary words for this lesson:

singular	appeared	aid	justice
composer	talents	legal	responds

▶▶▶▶ *There are four blank spaces in the story below. Four vocabulary words have already been used in the story. They are underlined. Use the other four words to fill in the blanks.*

Rubén Blades is a <u>composer</u> who was born in Panama. He sings his own salsa songs. These are not dance tunes. Blades has _____appeared_____ on stage to sing about the kind of world he would like to live in. In this world, all people would be treated fairly.

Blades has other _____talents_____. He is also an actor. Some of his movies include *The Milagro Beanfield War, The Two Jakes,* and *The Super.*

Blades is a lawyer, too. Sometimes people ask him <u>legal</u> questions. They know Blades can <u>aid</u> them with his advice. People listen carefully when he _____responds_____.

Years of hard work have made Blades famous. But he hasn't forgotten the people of Panama. He cares about their needs for <u>justice</u> and better living conditions. His songs have given them hope. Now he wants to do more. Rubén Blades is truly a _____singular_____ person.

Learn More About Panama

▶▶▶▶ *On a separate piece of paper or in your notebook or journal, complete one or more of the activities below.*

Learning Across the Curriculum

The Panama Canal, completed in 1914, changed the way ships traveled around the Americas. Research how the canal was created and draw a map that explains where the canal is.

Broadening Your Understanding

Imagine that Rubén Blades is running for president of Panama. Write a brief paragraph telling why you think people might or might not vote for him.

2 REBEL IN RHYTHM

The spotlight is on Twyla Tharp and the dancers. The dancers whirl like tops and tumble in **rotation.** While dancing, they look like the blinking colors in a neon sign. They move with the speed of light. The audience cheers. **Bouquets** of flowers are tossed on stage in honor of a great performance.

Twyla Tharp, the **rebel** of dance, has made it. She is one of America's **major** choreographers (kohree AHG raf erzs). Her job is to arrange the dances and direct the dancers. Tharp **combines** jazz and classical music in her work. Most of her dances are done on a plain stage with very little **scenery.** Sometimes she sets her dances to varied **background** music. But she doesn't always use music. Then all you hear are the dancers' breathing and the movements of their feet.

Tharp worked hard to become a world famous choreographer. As a teen, she put in long hours practicing her dance and music. She studied with many leading dancers. She believed there was a **grand** plan for her to become a star. Tharp's mother agreed that her daughter would be famous. She was so sure of this that she even changed the spelling of her daughter's name. *Twila* became *Twyla* because she thought it would look better in lights!

MAKE A LIST

>>>> *There are eight vocabulary words in this lesson. In the story, they are boxed in color. Copy the vocabulary words here.*

1. _____rotation_____   5. _____combines_____

2. _____bouquets_____   6. _____scenery_____

3. _____rebel_____   7. _____background_____

4. _____major_____   8. _____grand_____

MAKE AN ALPHABETICAL LIST

>>>> *Here are the eight words you copied on the previous page. Write them in alphabetical order in the spaces below.*

bouquets	scenery	rebel	combines
background	rotation	grand	major

1. _____ background _____

2. _____ bouquets _____

3. _____ combines _____

4. _____ grand _____

5. _____ major _____

6. _____ rebel _____

7. _____ rotation _____

8. _____ scenery _____

WHAT DO THE WORDS MEAN?

>>>> *Following are some meanings, or definitions, for the eight vocabulary words in this lesson. Write the words next to their definitions.*

1. _____ rebel _____ a person who goes against the system; one who resists authority

2. _____ grand _____ large; important; complete

3. _____ bouquets _____ bunches of flowers fastened together

4. _____ rotation _____ taking turns in a regular order; one following the other

5. _____ scenery _____ painted pictures or hangings for a stage

6. _____ combines _____ joins together; mixes

7. _____ major _____ main; principal

8. _____ background _____ accompanying the main action

It is important to know the vowels in the alphabet. They are *a, e, i, o, u,* and sometimes *y.*

When a vowel in a word has the same sound as its name, it is called a **long vowel.** The long vowel is marked by putting a line above the letter, like: ā, ē, ī, ō, ū.

Here are two samples of each of the long vowels.

long ā	**long ē**	**long ī**
cāke	wē	bīke
wāde	Pēte	fīre

long ō	**long ū**	**sometimes ȳ**
drōve	mūsic	happȳ (long e sound)
grōw	hūman	crȳ (long i sound)

Look at the following words. Underline the words that have long vowel sounds and put a line above the long vowel. The first one has been done as an example.

tūbe	bāby	store	pan	dīme

flop	claw	māde	īce	slōw

Underline each word in parentheses that has a long vowel sound. Then draw a line above the long vowel.

1. Did you get that (glove, rōbe) for your birthday?
2. I (māde, bought) a plane for my science class.
3. Lindbergh flew (swiftly, sōlo) across the Atlantic Ocean.
4. Would you like to be a (dancer, mūsician) one day?
5. Can you (rīde, sit) on your horse?
6. I'll race you to the (lāke, pond).

>>>> A **synonym** is a word that means the same, or nearly the same, as another word. *Happy* and *glad* are synonyms.

>>>> *The column on the left contains the eight key words in the story. To the right of each key word are three other words or groups of words. Two of these are synonyms for the key word. Circle the two synonyms.*

1. **bouquets**   green plants   (bunches of flowers)   (flowers tied together)

2. **major**   (principal)   serious   (main)

3. **rotation**   (taking turns)   speaking clearly   (one after another)

4. **scenery**   audience   (stage pictures)   (stage hangings)

5. **background**   future plans   (in the back)   (accompanying part)

6. **rebel**   (one who acts against authority)   one who joins the crowd   (one who goes against the system)

7. **combines**   separates   (joins)   (mixes)

8. **grand**   (important)   small   (large)

>>>> An **adjective** is a word that describes a person, place, or thing. For example, in the sentence, "Twyla Tharp is a talented dancer," *talented* is the word that describes *dancer*.

>>>> *Underline the adjectives in the sentences below.*

1. Twyla Tharp never expected to be a <u>famous</u> dancer.

2. Her dancers often perform on a <u>bare</u> stage with <u>simple</u> scenery.

3. After graduation, she continued studying with some of the <u>best</u> <u>dance</u> teachers.

4. A <u>good</u> dancer recognizes the value of an <u>excellent</u> teacher.

5. By combining jazz and <u>classical</u> ballet, Twyla has created <u>exciting</u> <u>new</u> dances.

>>>> *Look at the picture. What words come into your mind other than the ones you matched with their synonyms? Write them on the lines below. To help you get started, here are two good words:*

1. performers
2. dancing
3. Answers will vary.
4. _____

5. _____
6. _____
7. _____
8. _____

COMPLETE THE STORY

>>>> Here are the eight vocabulary words for this lesson:

rebel	combines	grand	rotation
background	scenery	major	bouquets

>>>> *There are four blank spaces in the story below. Four vocabulary words have already been used in the story. They are underlined. Use the other four words to fill in the blanks.*

Ballet has become an important art form in America. One of the people most responsible is Twyla Tharp. She has often been called a _____ rebel _____ because she does the unexpected. She combines jazz and classical ballet to form new routines. Sometimes she uses little or no scenery and no music. Her dancers perform unusual steps in rotation. They have been carefully trained by Tharp.

Tharp always believed there was a _____ grand _____ plan that pointed her toward stardom. Her plan was helped by her _____ background _____ and good training in dance and music. She studied musical instruments as well as most dance forms. She has also worked with some of the great dance teachers of our time.

Today Twyla Tharp is known as one of America's _____ major _____ choreographers. A choreographer is a person who creates dance movements. Tharp's dances are often greeted with applause and bouquets. She has given pleasure to millions of dance lovers.

Learn More About Dance

>>>> *On a separate piece of paper or in your notebook or journal, complete the activity below.*

Appreciating Diversity

In many cultures, dance isn't just for fun. It can be a celebration or part of an important ceremony. Research the history of a dance from another country. Explain what you learn to your class. If possible, let the class see the dance or hear the music to which the dance is performed.

3 UPSKIING

In winter, some people enjoy downhill skiing. After taking ski lifts to the top of snow-covered slopes, these skiers look forward to their thrilling and challenging **descents.** Other people prefer the less dangerous sport of cross-country skiing. Gliding along on mostly flat **terrain,** these skiers enjoy calmly viewing the wintery scene.

Some skiers seek the greater challenge of skiing down very high, very **remote,** and very dangerous mountains. They do not, however, enjoy the hours it takes them to climb to the summits. These **venturesome** people have been trying out a new sport called upskiing. Upskiers use **expensive,** custom-made parachutes to get to mountain peaks. Once there, the skiers fold their parachutes into backpacks and ski down the slope.

Intrigued by this unusual sport, a television crew went to film upskiers on Wrangell Mountain in eastern Alaska. This mountain is known for its raging storms, dangerous crevasses, and zero **visibility.** An air taxi took the crew to a glacier at 9,000 feet. Although the summit was only 5,163 feet above them, the crew had to wait for 15 days until the weather was just right. Finally, a good breeze came and the skies cleared. The skiers were **ecstatic.** They were now able to ski uphill at 3.5 miles per hour to reach their mountain-peak destination!

MAKE A LIST

>>>> *There are eight vocabulary words in this lesson. In the story, they are boxed in color. Copy the vocabulary words here.*

1. _____ descents _____   5. _____ expensive _____

2. _____ terrain _____   6. _____ intrigued _____

3. _____ remote _____   7. _____ visibility _____

4. _____ venturesome _____   8. _____ ecstatic _____

MAKE AN ALPHABETICAL LIST

>>>> *Here are the eight words you copied on the previous page. Write them in alphabetical order in the spaces below.*

descents	expensive	terrain	intrigued
remote	visibility	venturesome	ecstatic

1. descents

2. ecstatic

3. expensive

4. intrigued

5. remote

6. terrain

7. venturesome

8. visibility

WHAT DO THE WORDS MEAN?

>>>> *Following are some meanings, or definitions, for the eight vocabulary words in this lesson. Write the words next to their definitions.*

1. expensive — costly; high-priced

2. intrigued — interested; aroused by curiosity

3. remote — faraway; unsettled

4. descents — downward passages

5. terrain — the ground

6. visibility — ability to see

7. ecstatic — very happy or joyful

8. venturesome — seeking adventure; daring; bold

>>>> There are 26 letters in the alphabet. Twenty-one letters including the letter *y* are called consonants. Five letters (*a, e, i, o, u*) and sometimes *y* are called vowels.

Consonants appear at the beginning, at the end, and in the middle of words. Consonants that appear in the middle are called medial consonants. For example, in the word *hammer,*

h	is a beginning consonant
mm	are the medial consonants
r	is a final consonant

>>>> Here are ten words. See how well you can recognize the beginning, medial, and final consonants. Each word in the list contains consonants. Some have beginning consonants. Some have medial consonants. Some have final consonants. Some may have all three types of consonants.

>>>> *Check each word for all three consonant positions. Then write the consonants in each word in the correct list. The first one has been done as an example.*

	Beginning	Medial	Final
1. kitten	k	tt	n
2. hoped	h	p	d
3. actor		ct	r
4. corner	c	rn	r
5. each			ch
6. dancing	d	nc	ng
7. disco	d	sc	
8. umpire		mp	r

>>>> A **synonym** is a word that means the same, or nearly the same, as another word. *Happy* and *glad* are synonyms.

>>>> *The column on the left contains the eight key words in the story. To the right of each key word are three other words or groups of words. Two of these are synonyms for the key word. Circle the two synonyms.*

1. **descents** (downward passages) mountains (ways down)

2. **terrain** (land) (ground) climate

3. **remote** populated (faraway) (unsettled)

4. **venturesome** scared (bold) (daring)

5. **expensive** (costly) (high priced) cheap

6. **intrigued** (interested) (curious) uninterested

7. **visibility** (what can be seen) air pressure (ability to view)

8. **ecstatic** (very joyful) sad (extremely happy)

>>>> *These five sentences have been scrambled or mixed up. Write the words in the correct order so that they make complete sentences.*

1. popular winter is sport a skiing

Skiing is a popular winter sport.

2. to upskiers mountain parachutes use help peaks reach

Upskiers use parachutes to help reach mountain peaks.

3. parachutes descents tucked backpacks the are into for

The parachutes are tucked into backpacks for descents.

4. breeze needed to parachutes work a is for the strong

A strong breeze is needed for the parachutes to work.

5. most only skiers enjoy the upskiing daring

Only the most daring skiers enjoy upskiing.

>>>> *Look at the picture. What words come into your mind other than the ones you just matched with their synonyms? Write them on the lines below. To help you get started, here are two good words:*

1. _____ parachute _____
2. _____ uphill _____
3. ___ Answers will vary. ___
4. _____

5. _____
6. _____
7. _____
8. _____

24

COMPLETE THE STORY

>>>> Here are the eight vocabulary words for this lesson:

| descents | expensive | terrain | intrigued |
| remote | visibility | venturesome | ecstatic |

>>>> *There are four blank spaces in the story below. Four vocabulary words have already been used in the story. They are underlined. Use the other four words to fill in the blanks.*

It's good to know that there are some new sports that people are just discovering. Upskiing is one of them.

Even in the 1990s, there are mountains that have never been skied down. These mountains are usually far from cities, in _____ remote _____ areas. Upskiers are intrigued by the challenges that these mountains present. The slopes are often ice covered with deep crevasses. The fog can be so thick that the _____ visibility _____ is zero. Upskiers risk their lives traveling to the mountain peaks and then skiing down the rugged terrain.

To reach the mountain peaks, these venturesome skiers use specially made, expensive parachutes. When a strong breeze comes and helps lift them up the mountain, the skiers feel _____ ecstatic _____. Some skiers enjoy going up mountains more than they enjoy the _____ descents _____.

Learn More About Skiing

>>>> *On a separate piece of paper or in your notebook or journal, complete one or more of the activities below.*

Broadening Your Understanding
People who are active in very cold weather have to be careful. Research the health problems that can occur in the mountains in winter. Write about the dangers these adventurers face. Then write some advice you would give them about being safe during their activity.

Learning Across the Curriculum
Avalanches are one danger that winter sports-lovers face. Find out what causes an avalanche. Explain the process to your class. Make a diagram to show to the class during your presentation.

4 AN AMERICAN FIRST

Many politicians have had simple childhoods. Many have had to work their way through school. Why, then, is L. Douglas Wilder unusual? He is the first African American governor of Virginia and the first African American governor in the United States.

Wilder was born in 1931 in Richmond, the **capital** of Virginia. His parents worked hard, and the family was not rich. In fact, his grandparents had been slaves. Wilder finished college and fought in the Korean War in the early 1950s. He **objected** when the African American members of his **outfit** did not receive promotions. Shortly afterward, African Americans, including Wilder, began to receive promotions. After his time in the army, he went to law school and became a successful Richmond lawyer.

He went into politics in the early 1970s, during the civil rights movement in Virginia. Remembering his army days, he often spoke out angrily about the **limits** that blocked African Americans in his state.

Wilder's personality has seemed to **undergo** a change in the past few years. He is interested in working with his **opponents.** He is **hailed** as a person who can make good things happen. He serves as a fine **example** for others who want to serve their country.

MAKE A LIST

>>>> *There are eight vocabulary words in this lesson. In the story, they are boxed in color. Copy the vocabulary words here.*

1. _capital_
2. _objected_
3. _outfit_
4. _limits_

5. _undergo_
6. _opponents_
7. _hailed_
8. _example_

MAKE AN ALPHABETICAL LIST

>>>> *Here are the eight words you copied on the previous page. Write them in alphabetical order in the spaces below.*

capital	undergo	objected	opponents
outfit	hailed	limits	example

1. _capital_
2. _example_
3. _hailed_
4. _limits_

5. _objected_
6. _opponents_
7. _outfit_
8. _undergo_

WHAT DO THE WORDS MEAN?

>>>> *Following are some meanings, or definitions, for the eight vocabulary words in this lesson. Write the words next to their definitions.*

1. _hailed_   praised; saluted
2. _undergo_   to experience; to go through
3. _example_   a model
4. _capital_   the city where government meets
5. _outfit_   a group; a team
6. _objected_   spoke out against; protested
7. _opponents_   enemies; those who disagree
8. _limits_   borders; stopping places

>>>> **Digraphs** are two consonants or vowels that make a single sound. They can appear at the beginning, middle, and end of words. In this lesson, you will work with beginning consonant digraphs.

Here are some examples of beginning consonant digraphs.

ch	sh	kn	th	wh	wr
chip	shine	knew	thin	when	wrong
child	shoe	knife	this	where	write

>>>> *The following sentences contain incomplete words that can be completed by using a beginning consonant digraph. Read each sentence carefully. Decide which of the digraphs listed above is needed for each underlined word. Then write the digraphs next to each incomplete word. The first one has been done as an example.*

1. The wagon won't work because a **wh**eel came off.

2. How do you like my new gold _____chain_____?

3. Did your dog catch the ball you _____threw_____?

4. My toes hurt because my _____shoes_____ are too tight.

5. _____Three_____ is my lucky number. Do you _____know_____ yours?

6. No matter how hard I try, I still can't _____whistle_____.

7. The juice will stay cold if you pour it into a _____thermos_____.

8. Does your family go to _____church_____ services?

9. He had five _____wrong_____ answers, so he failed the test.

10. Do you know the story of Moby Dick, the _____white_____ _____whale_____?

>>>> A **synonym** is a word that means the same, or nearly the same, as another word. *Happy* and *glad* are synonyms.

>>>> *The column on the left contains the eight key words in the story. To the right of each key word are three other words or groups of words. Two of these are synonyms for the key word. Circle the two synonyms.*

1.	**objected**	(protested)	(argued)	agreed
2.	**limits**	(borders)	coverings	(barriers)
3.	**undergo**	receive	(live through)	(experience)
4.	**hailed**	(praised)	attacked	(supported)
5.	**capital**	(governing city)	largest city	(government center)
6.	**example**	action	(model)	(sample)
7.	**opponents**	(enemies)	friends	(rivals)
8.	**outfit**	(group)	outing	(team)

>>>> There are many words in our language that are often misspelled. These words are spelled incorrectly so many times that they are sometimes called *spelling demons*. (A demon is a devil, or an evil spirit, and these words cause a great deal of trouble.)

>>>> *Here are some words that cause trouble. There is a correct spelling and an incorrect one. Underline the correct spelling. Then write out each correct word on the blank lines. The first one has been done as an example.*

		Correct Spelling
<u>receive</u>	recieve	receive
sucess	<u>success</u>	success
<u>pleasant</u>	pleasent	pleasant
<u>certain</u>	certin	certain
seperate	<u>separate</u>	separate
<u>benefit</u>	benifit	benefit
discribe	<u>describe</u>	describe

31

USE YOUR OWN WORDS

>>>> *Look at the picture. What words come into your mind other than the ones you just matched with their synonyms? Write them on the lines below. To help you get started, here are two good words:*

1. _____ ceremony _____   5. _____

2. _____ governor _____   6. _____

3. _____ Answers will vary. _____   7. _____

4. _____   8. _____

32

>>>> Here are the eight vocabulary words for this lesson:

capital	undergo	objected	opponents
outfit	hailed	limits	example

>>>> *Four vocabulary words have been used in the story below. They are underlined. Use the four other vocabulary words to fill in the blanks.*

L. Douglas Wilder is proud of his Virginia background. Wilder was born in the _____capital_____ of Virginia. His childhood was not easy. He learned early about the _____limits_____ placed on African American people. When he joined the army, he faced another problem. He <u>objected</u> when African Americans were not given promotions. His commanding officer agreed with him. He and other members of his army _____outfit_____ were given promotions after his complaints.

Wilder is a flexible politician. He is willing to <u>undergo</u> changes in his approach to government. He used to argue with his enemies, but he has learned to cooperate with his _____opponents_____. This new attitude gets things done. His willingness to work with others has been <u>hailed</u> by many people. He is an <u>example</u> of the new politician whom others will copy.

Learn More About Politicians

>>>> *On a separate piece of paper or in your notebook or journal, complete one or more of the activities below.*

Broadening Your Understanding

Research the issues that people in your community feel are important. Then imagine you are running for public office in your area. What issues will you focus on? Write your campaign platform in which you tell people what you will do if elected.

Learning Across the Curriculum

Find out about the history of African Americans in politics in the United States. Make a time line of important events for African Americans in politics. Include such events as the year African Americans got the right to vote and the election of the first African American representative or senator.

5 HIGH FLYER

At the age of 14, Tito Gaona saw a movie. It changed his life. The movie was *Trapeze* with Burt Lancaster and Tony Curtis. Curtis played an **aerialist** who wanted to do the "triple." The triple is three **somersaults** in midair off a swinging **trapeze.** This movie inspired Gaona. He made up his mind to become a trapeze artist.

He practiced with his father, Vincent, a former **acrobat.** Vincent became his "catcher." The catcher is the person who grasps the flyer as he completes the movements. At the age of 18, Gaona was doing the "triple" in the circus. Only four persons had done the triple before Gaona. Two of them died from broken necks while performing.

During the **stunt,** Gaona moves at an **incredible** speed. He travels at 75 miles an hour. If Gaona lands on his neck, he could break it. He has only a **fraction** of a second to **tuck** his neck in. Then he has to land on his back in the net.

One day Gaona completed the "quadruple." His catcher caught him. But it was just practice. There were no cameras or spectators to see him do it. Someday, he'll do it under the Big Top, and thousands will be watching.

MAKE A LIST

>>>> *There are eight vocabulary words in this lesson. In the story, they are boxed in color. Copy the vocabulary words here.*

1. _____ aerialist _____   5. _____ stunt _____

2. _____ somersaults _____   6. _____ incredible _____

3. _____ trapeze _____   7. _____ fraction _____

4. _____ acrobat _____   8. _____ tuck _____

35

MAKE AN ALPHABETICAL LIST

>>>> *Here are the eight words you copied on the previous page. Write them in alphabetical order in the spaces below.*

trapeze	acrobat	tuck	aerialist
somersaults	fraction	stunt	incredible

1. _____acrobat_____   5. _____somersaults_____

2. _____aerialist_____   6. _____stunt_____

3. _____fraction_____   7. _____trapeze_____

4. _____incredible_____   8. _____tuck_____

WHAT DO THE WORDS MEAN?

>>>> *Following are some meanings, or definitions, for the eight vocabulary words in this lesson. Write the words next to their definitions.*

1. _____aerialist_____ a person who performs on a trapeze; a flyer

2. _____somersaults_____ full body turns, forward or backward

3. _____tuck_____ to pull in; to draw in closely

4. _____stunt_____ a daring trick; a display of skill

5. _____fraction_____ a small part; less than a second in time

6. _____trapeze_____ a short horizontal bar, hung by two ropes, on which aerialists perform

7. _____acrobat_____ a skilled gymnast; an expert in tumbling

8. _____incredible_____ almost impossible to believe

>>>> Once again, let's look at some words that have short vowel sounds. For example, *cap, hop, rip*. Now add *e* to each of these words. Look at the new words: *cape, hope, ripe*. Notice that each of the new words now has the *long* vowel in the middle and the final *e* is silent. A silent *e* at the end of a one-syllable word makes the vowel long.

>>>> *Here is a list of words containing the short vowel sound. Make new words by adding an e to the end of each word. Then write the new words on the lines provided. Pronounce each new word to yourself. It should have the long vowel sound. The first one has been done as an example.*

cop	cope	hug	huge
pip	pipe	strip	stripe
past	paste	cut	cute
pan	pane	fad	fade
dim	dime	hop	hope
slop	slope	pin	pine
cub	cube	rat	rate
kit	kite	rid	ride
mad	made	spin	spine
bit	bite	fat	fate

>>>> A **synonym** is a word that means the same, or nearly the same, as another word. *Happy* and *glad* are synonyms.

>>>> *The column on the left contains the eight key words in the story. To the right of each key word are three other words or groups of words. Two of these are synonyms for the key word. Circle the two synonyms.*

1. **incredible**   (amazing)   (unbelievable)   ordinary

2. **somersaults**   circus foods   (acrobatic tricks)   (full body turns)

3. **tuck**   to unfold   (to pull in)   (to draw together)

4. **aerialist**   (a circus flyer)   a ringmaster   (a performer on a trapeze)

5. **stunt**   (a clever trick)   a stupid idea   (a daring feat)

6. **acrobat**   (an expert gymnast)   (a skilled tumbler)   an animal trainer

7. **trapeze**   a circular cage   (a swing for aerialists)   (a bar hung from two ropes)

8. **fraction**   (a small part)   (a tiny piece)   the total

>>>> Many words end in *ed*, *er*, or *ing*. These endings can change the meaning of a word or form a new word.

>>>> *Add the correct ending to the word before each sentence. Then write the new word in the blank space. Remember: sometimes you drop the final* e *before adding the* ed, er, *or* ing. *The first one has been done as an example.*

1. **tuck**   He ___tucked___ his neck in before hitting the net.

2. **catch**   The ___catcher___ must grasp the aerialist's forearms.

3. **watch**   Someday, he will succeed, and thousands will be ___watching___.

4. **move**   The aerialist is ___moving___ through the air at an incredible speed.

5. **complete**   To date, no one has ___completed___ the quadruple in public.

6. **change**   The movie *Trapeze* ___changed___ his life.

7. **announce**   The ___announcer___ asked the crowd to be quiet.

8. **somersault** Maria felt wonderful as she ___somersaulted___ through the air.

39

>>>> *Look at the picture. What words come into your mind other than the ones you just matched with their synonyms? Write them on the lines below. To help you get started, here are two good words:*

1. _____ropes_____   5. _____

2. _____flying_____   6. _____

3. ___Answers will vary.___   7. _____

4. _____   8. _____

COMPLETE THE STORY

>>>> Here are the eight vocabulary words for this lesson:

aerialist	trapeze	tuck	incredible
stunt	somersaults	acrobat	fraction

>>>> *There are four blank spaces in the story below. Four vocabulary words have already been used in the story. They are underlined. Use the other four words to fill in the blanks.*

There are many popular circus acts. Each has its own special appeal. But when an aerialist starts to climb to the ___trapeze___, all the other acts stop. These high flyers become the center of all eyes. Even though there is a net below, the risk is still there. Flying through the air at an ___incredible___ speed does not allow for errors. A failure to tuck in one's head can cause serious injury.

One of the most amazing performers is Tito Gaona. He has made the triple a regular part of his act. Now he is working on the quadruple. It is not just an ordinary stunt. This stunt involves four back ___somersaults___ in midair. Only the most skilled acrobat could think of trying it. It requires skill, strength, and timing. If the flyer is only a ___fraction___ off the mark, it can mean a rough tumble to the net—and more practice!

Learn More About the Circus

>>>> *On a separate piece of paper or in your notebook or journal, complete one or more of the activities below.*

Broadening Your Understanding
Circuses change as people's tastes change. Find out about some acts that circuses feature and create a circus for the future. Draw a picture of your circus.

Extending Your Reading
Circuses have a long history. Read one of these books about the circus and write why you think circuses have been so popular throughout history.

The Big Show, by Felix Sutton
The Circus, by Mary Kay Phelan
Old Bet and the Start of the American Circus, by Robert McClung

6 NOBEL PRIZE WINNER

Rosalyn Yalow is the second woman to win the Nobel Prize in medicine. She's a scientist from New York City. She works 80 hours a week. Yalow feels she must work harder than men to **achieve** success. She says, "It's a man's world." But she's trying to change that.

Yalow worked out a way to measure **substances** in the blood and tissue. It doesn't matter how small the substance is. Her method can measure it. This method helps **detect** disease early.

In college, Yalow won high honors in science. After college, she applied for a job as a teacher's aid. But she was **rejected** because she was a woman. Even after this defeat, she was **resolved** to win. She said, "I'm going to show the world a woman can succeed."

Finally, the University of Illinois **admitted** her to medical school. Yalow worked and studied there until graduation. Then she returned to New York City where jobs were **plentiful.** Yalow got a job in a hospital. There, she began her **inquiries** into ways to help people. That was more than 40 years ago. She's still in New York City today, working to discover more cures for disease.

Rosalyn Yalow, super scientist, is a super woman!

MAKE A LIST

>>>> *There are eight vocabulary words in this lesson. In the story, they are boxed in color. Copy the vocabulary words here.*

1. achieve
2. substances
3. detect
4. rejected
5. resolved
6. admitted
7. plentiful
8. inquiries

43

MAKE AN ALPHABETICAL LIST

>>>> *Here are the eight words you copied on the previous page. Write them in alphabetical order in the spaces below.*

| admitted | substances | detect | resolved |
| achieve | plentiful | inquiries | rejected |

1. achieve
2. admitted
3. detect
4. inquiries
5. plentiful
6. rejected
7. resolved
8. substances

WHAT DO THE WORDS MEAN?

>>>> *Following are some meanings, or definitions, for the eight vocabulary words in this lesson. Write the words next to their definitions.*

1. detect — to discover; to find out
2. achieve — to reach a desired goal
3. inquiries — questions
4. substances — materials from which something is made
5. resolved — determined; fixed in purpose
6. rejected — refused or turned away
7. plentiful — more than enough; abundant
8. admitted — gave permission to enroll as a student; allowed to enter

>>>> **Blends** are the sounds of two or three consonants that come together at the beginning, middle, or end of words. You will study some beginning blends in this lesson.

Here are some examples of beginning consonant blends:

bl	br	cl	cr	dr
blend	brag	clown	crook	drop
fl	**gr**	**spr**	**str**	
flag	grass	spread	stroke	

>>>> *Complete the following sentences by supplying a word that begins with a consonant blend. For example, "The synonym for **happy** is _____." The answer must begin with a blend. The answer is **glad**. The first one has been done as an example.*

1. One of the _____blades_____ on her new pair of skates was bent.

2. He tried to catch the mouse in his new _____trap_____.

3. A word that means the opposite of *back* is _____front_____.

4. A farmer plants seeds to get a _____crop_____.

5. A circus comic is called a _____clown_____.

6. The picture was too small for the _____frame_____.

7. Before you mail a letter, make sure it has a _____stamp_____.

8. She felt pretty in her new _____dress_____.

9. After the race, he looked forward to a big _____glass_____ of cold milk.

10. Our English _____class_____ ended early today.

FIND THE SYNONYMS

>>>> A **synonym** is a word that means the same, or nearly the same, as another word. *Happy* and *glad* are synonyms.

>>>> *The column on the left contains the eight key words in the story. To the right of each key word are three other words or groups of words. Two of these are synonyms for the key word. Circle the two synonyms.*

1. **inquiries** (questions) motions (investigations)

2. **detect** (to find out) to hate (to discover)

3. **rejected** lost (turned away) (refused)

4. **achieve** (to do well) to fail (to reach a goal)

5. **plentiful** few (more than enough) (a great many)

6. **admitted** (accepted) refused (allowed in)

7. **substances** (materials) (kinds of matter) thoughts

8. **resolved** changed (decided) (determined)

>>>> **Antonyms** are words that are opposite in meaning. For example, *good/bad* and *fast/slow* are antonyms. Below are antonyms for six of the vocabulary words.

>>>> *See if you can find the vocabulary words and write them in the blank spaces on the left. The first one has been done as an example.*

Vocabulary Word	Antonym
1. resolved	undecided
2. achieve	fail
3. plentiful	scarce
4. rejected	accepted
5. admitted	refused entrance
6. inquiries	answers

USE YOUR OWN WORDS

>>>> *Look at the picture. What words come into your mind other than the ones you just matched with their synonyms? Write them on the lines below. To help you get started, here are two good words:*

1. _____handshake_____   5. _____

2. _____medals_____   6. _____

3. ____Answers will vary.____   7. _____

4. _____   8. _____

COMPLETE THE STORY

>>>> Here are the eight vocabulary words for this lesson:

achieve	inquiries	detect	rejected
resolved	substances	admitted	plentiful

>>>> *There are four blank spaces in the story below. Four vocabulary words have already been used in the story. They are underlined. Use the other four words to fill in the blanks.*

Marie Curie was the first woman to win the Nobel Prize for her medical <u>inquiries</u>. That happened in 1911. Sixty-six years later, the prize was awarded to Rosalyn Yalow. She had found a new way of measuring _____substances_____ in the blood. Any discovery that can <u>detect</u> disease early deserves a prize. Many lives have been saved because of Yalow's work.

Yalow came from a poor family. But her parents _____resolved_____ that their daughter would have a better life. They knew the importance of education. Yalow never forgot their advice. She was determined to <u>achieve</u> results.

After college, Yalow applied to many universities to be a teacher's aid. She was <u>rejected</u> because she was a woman. Finally, the University of Illinois _____admitted_____ her. Later she returned to New York for a job. Jobs were _____plentiful_____ at that time.

Learn More About Nobel Prizes

>>>> *On a separate piece of paper or in your notebook or journal, complete one or more of the activities below.*

Learning Across the Curriculum

Research the discoveries of a scientist who has won a Nobel prize. Then explain to your class why the scientist earned the award and how his or her research has helped people.

Broadening Your Understanding

Imagine you are on the committee that will decide the winner of this year's Nobel Peace Prize. Decide who you believe deserves the award for this year. Write a speech explaining why you are nominating this person. You may want to do some research to gather reasons why this person deserves the award.

7 WALKING HIGH STEEL

"Look out! Steel beam coming up!" the **foreman** called. Jim Tallchief climbed the steel structure with the **skill** of a cat. Quickly, he worked his way from beam to beam. He balanced himself with **ease.** Tallchief was **alert.** He grasped the rising beam and fastened it in place.

Jim Tallchief is a Mohawk, a member of the Iroquois nation. He is proud of his Native American ancestry. Because they are so sure-footed, Mohawks are the most **agile** steelworkers in the world. Much of their labor is done in small groups. The work is very dangerous, so it is important that they cooperate with one another. Each member of the group must know that the other members will be alert under pressure.

In 1907, a bridge **collapsed** before it was finished. It caused the death of 35 Mohawks. Many women became **widows.** Strangely enough, the risk made the work more attractive to some of the Native Americans. But large groups no longer work on the same dangerous **construction** project. Now one accident cannot cause harm to so many people.

The life of a steelworker is hard. The workers are proud of their deeds. They feel that to excel on the high beam is to prove oneself.

MAKE A LIST

>>>> *There are eight vocabulary words in this lesson. In the story, they are boxed in color. Copy the vocabulary words here.*

1. _____ foreman _____   5. _____ agile _____

2. _____ skill _____   6. _____ collapsed _____

3. _____ ease _____   7. _____ widows _____

4. _____ alert _____   8. _____ construction _____

MAKE AN ALPHABETICAL LIST

>>>> Here are the eight words you copied on the previous page. Write them in alphabetical order in the spaces below.

alert	construction	collapsed	agile
widows	skill	foreman	ease

1. _____agile_____   5. _____ease_____

2. _____alert_____   6. _____foreman_____

3. _____collapsed_____   7. _____skill_____

4. _____construction_____   8. _____widows_____

WHAT DO THE WORDS MEAN?

>>>> Following are some meanings, or definitions, for the eight vocabulary words in this lesson. Write the words next to their definitions.

1. _____collapsed_____ broke down suddenly; fell down

2. _____alert_____ quick in thought and action; watchful

3. _____construction_____ the process of building

4. _____widows_____ women whose husbands have died

5. _____agile_____ having quick, easy movements; limber

6. _____skill_____ the ability to use one's knowledge in doing something

7. _____foreman_____ a person in charge of a group of workers; a boss

8. _____ease_____ a natural way or manner

52

>>>> Words have rhythm. They are divided into syllables like musical beats in a song or dance. If you understand syllables, your spelling and pronunciation will improve. Say the following words slowly and clap for each syllable as you say them.

climb	=	one syllable
climb ing	=	two syllables
po ta to	=	three syllables
im poss i ble	=	four syllables

Here is a short rule to keep in mind. For each syllable, there must be a vowel sound.

>>>> *Look at the following list of words. Write the number of vowels in each word. Then say the word and listen for the number of vowel sounds. The number of vowel sounds you hear will be the number of syllables in the word. The first one has been done as an example.*

	Number of Vowels	Vowel Sounds	Syllables
drive	2	1	1
suitcase	4	2	2
microfilm	3	3	3
motorcycle	4	4	4
football	3	2	2
track	1	1	1
basketball	3	3	3
runner	2	2	2

>>>> A **synonym** is a word that means the same, or nearly the same, as another word. *Happy* and *glad* are synonyms.

>>>> *The column on the left contains the eight key words in the story. To the right of each key word are three other words or groups of words. Two of these are synonyms for the key word. Circle the two synonyms.*

1. **foreman**   (a boss)   an assistant   (a person in charge)

2. **skill**   (ability)   (knowledge)   fear

3. **ease**   (comfort)   stress   (relaxation)

4. **alert**   lazy   (watchful)   (quick in thought)

5. **collapsed**   (gave way)   (fell down)   held together

6. **construction**   (the process of building)   a style of painting   (a manner of building)

7. **agile**   (coordinated)   clumsy   (quick)

8. **widows**   (women who lost their husbands through death)   divorced women   (women whose husbands have died)

>>>> Some words are often confused because they look alike or sound alike. For example, *there/their* and *where/wear* are often confused.

>>>> *Place the correct word in each of the blank spaces in the following sentences.*

1. **picture, pitcher**   In my baseball scrapbook, I have a ____picture____ of my favorite ____pitcher____.

2. **lose, loose**   Because my top button is ____loose____, I will probably ____lose____ it.

3. **wait, weight**   The woman had to ____wait____ in line before the doctor could check her ____weight____.

4. **would, wood**   If we started to chop now, we ____would____ have enough ____wood____ for the entire winter.

5. **passed, past**   For the ____past____ three years, I have ____passed____ every examination that has come my way.

6. **meat, meet**   Tell your mother I will ____meet____ her in front of the ____meat____ counter.

55

>>>> *Look at the picture. What words come into your mind other than the ones you just matched with their synonyms? Write them on the lines below. To help you get started, here are two good words:*

1. _____water_____   5. _____

2. _____height_____   6. _____

3. ___Answers will vary.___   7. _____

4. _____   8. _____

COMPLETE THE STORY

▶▶▶▶ Here are the eight vocabulary words for this lesson:

widows	construction	agile	foreman
skill	collapsed	ease	alert

▶▶▶▶ *There are four blank spaces in the story below. Four vocabulary words have already been used in the story. They are underlined. Use the other four words to fill in the blanks.*

Steelworkers are special people. It takes unusual <u>skill</u> and courage to walk high beams. If one is not <u>alert</u>, lives may be in danger. Among the most _____agile_____ steelworkers are Mohawks. They have been doing this work for many years. When a high bridge is under <u>construction</u>, the _____foreman_____ looks for workers he can rely on. They must be surefooted and dependable. They must also cooperate with <u>ease</u>.

Work on high beams is not without great loss. In 1907, a bridge _____collapsed_____ and caused the death of 35 Mohawks. This left many women as _____widows_____. This disaster did not stop the others from working. But now, smaller groups work on dangerous projects. An accident will not cause many brave people to be lost.

Learn More About Native Americans

▶▶▶▶ *On a separate piece of paper or in your notebook or journal, complete one or more of the activities below.*

Working Together

Have each member of your group research the location of an Indian tribe's land. Find out the kinds of activities that were important to the people. Then have the group make a map showing the locations of the different tribes. Each member should explain to the class how the people's activities are related to the geographic area where they lived.

Learning Across the Curriculum

Use a copy of a state map to locate and identify the Native American reservations in your state or a state in which you are interested. Find out who lives on the reservations and what percentage of the state's land belongs to the Native Americans.

8 BORN TO WRITE

Gary Soto knows the meaning of poverty. He knows what it is like to grow up in a world filled with hardship. Soto grew up in California. For a while, his home was the world of migrant farm workers. He worked as a field hand. He put in long hours *harvesting* crops. Like other field hands, he was paid low wages. Also like other farm workers, his family was poor. They could not *afford* a nice home or new clothes. They often had to *accept* charity to get by.

Today Soto writes about his past. His books and poems often tell about things that really happened to him. One of his stories is about a boy who wore an ugly *jacket* to school. The boy was *ashamed* of the jacket. The color *reminded* him of dark green mush. But his mother said he had to wear it. The boy felt so bad that he got a D on a math test. He was so *upset* he even forgot the names of the state capitals.

Through his writings, Soto shows readers what it is like to be a Mexican American. He gives readers a view of what many Chicanos *experience* in fields and factories. These views are not often written about. They are not a part of the world seen on television and in the daily news. However, they are about real people who know that Gary Soto speaks honestly.

MAKE A LIST

>>>> *There are eight vocabulary words in this lesson. In the story, they are boxed in color. Copy the vocabulary words here.*

1. _____harvesting_____
2. _____afford_____
3. _____accept_____
4. _____jacket_____

5. _____ashamed_____
6. _____reminded_____
7. _____upset_____
8. _____experience_____

MAKE AN ALPHABETICAL LIST

>>>> *Here are the eight words you copied on the previous page. Write them in alphabetical order in the spaces below.*

harvesting	ashamed	accept	jacket
upset	afford	experience	reminded

1. _____accept_____
2. _____afford_____
3. _____ashamed_____
4. _____experience_____

5. _____harvesting_____
6. _____jacket_____
7. _____reminded_____
8. _____upset_____

WHAT DO THE WORDS MEAN?

>>>> *Following are some meanings, or definitions, for the eight vocabulary words in this lesson. Write the words next to their definitions.*

1. _____ashamed_____ embarrassed; feeling shame
2. _____upset_____ distressed; disturbed
3. _____reminded_____ thought of something again
4. _____harvesting_____ gathering of crops
5. _____experience_____ the act of living through an event
6. _____afford_____ to have the ability to purchase something
7. _____jacket_____ short coat
8. _____accept_____ to agree to take or receive

>>>> When you join one whole word with another whole word, a new single word is formed. This new word is called a **compound word**. For example, when you put the two words *air* and *plane* together, you get *airplane*. Here are three more examples.

steam + ship =	steamship
bed + room =	bedroom
cow + boy =	cowboy

>>>> *Draw lines from Column A to Column B to form new compound words.*

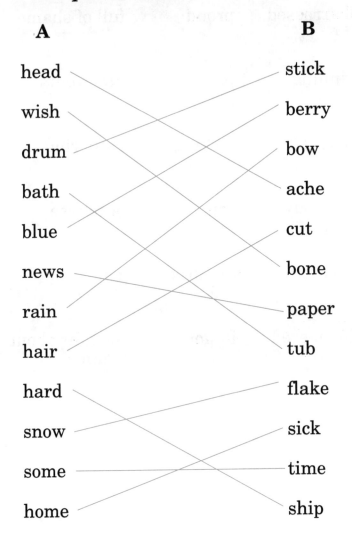

A	B
head	stick
wish	berry
drum	bow
bath	ache
blue	cut
news	bone
rain	paper
hair	tub
hard	flake
snow	sick
some	time
home	ship

FIND THE SYNONYMS

>>>> A **synonym** is a word that means the same, or nearly the same, as another word. *Happy* and *glad* are synonyms.

>>>> *The column on the left contains the eight key words in the story. To the right of each key word are three other words or groups of words. Two of these are synonyms for the key word. Circle the two synonyms.*

1. **jacket** (short coat) pocket (outer covering)

2. **accept** refuse (receive) (agree to take)

3. **ashamed** (embarrassed) proud (full of shame)

4. **experience** beginning (past) (life events)

5. **harvesting** planting (picking) (gathering)

6. **afford** (able to buy) sell (purchase)

7. **upset** (distressed) (disturbed) calm

8. **reminded** (remembered) forgot (thought about again)

>>>> Many times two words are shortened into one by leaving out one or more letters and putting in an apostrophe. The shortened word is called a **contraction**. For example, *I'll* is the contraction for *I will*. *Don't* is the contraction for *do not*.

>>>> *In the left-hand column are the two words that form the contraction. Write the contraction in the right-hand column.*

Contraction

1. they are — they're

2. you are — you're

3. does not — doesn't

4. who is — who's

5. you have — you've

6. it is — it's

7. you will — you'll

8. have not — haven't

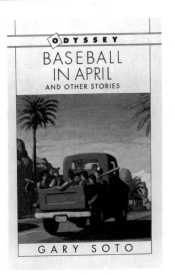

LoCal NeWS

by Gary Soto

USE YOUR OWN WORDS

>>>> *Look at the picture. What words come into your mind other than the ones you matched with their synonyms? Write them on the lines below. To help you get started, here are two good words:*

1. _____Chicano_____   5. _____

2. _____family_____   6. _____

3. _Answers will vary._   7. _____

4. _____   8. _____

>>>> Here are the eight vocabulary words for this lesson:

harvesting	ashamed	afford	upset
accept	reminded	jacket	experience

>>>> *There are four blank spaces in the story below. Four vocabulary words have already been used in the story. They are underlined. Use the other four words to fill in the blanks.*

Gary Soto once worked as a farmhand. He spent many hours ___harvesting___ crops. He received little pay for his work. He could not ___afford___ to buy new things. Even a nice <u>jacket</u> was beyond his means!

Gary Soto is not <u>ashamed</u> of his past. He has used this ___experience___ to become a popular author. He writes about life as a Mexican American.

Schools invite Soto to come and speak with their students. He does <u>accept</u> their invitations. He is ___reminded___ of himself when he meets Chicano children. He tells the students about his life. The students discover how <u>upset</u> Soto was living a life of poverty. But they also discover that people can make better lives for themselves. The students realize that it is possible for a poor farm worker to one day become a famous author.

Learn More About Migrant Farming

>>>> *On a separate piece of paper or in your notebook or journal, complete one or more of the activities below.*

Appreciating Diversity

Imagine that your parents are migrant farmers. Your family has moved three times during the past year. Write a letter to a friend that describes your experiences.

Learning Across the Curriculum

The need for migrant farmers is based upon a crop's growing season. Use references to determine the growing seasons of a few states. Make a travel schedule for a farmer who wants to work all 12 months of the year. Write the time of year, identify the states the farmer should go to, and list the types of crops the farmer would be working with.

9 THE GREY CUP

The United States has the Super Bowl. Canada has the Grey Cup. Both games are lively. Without **debating** the good points of each, most people agree that the Grey Cup **arouses** more interest. The whole country takes part. It is more than a game. People celebrate. It is a **mixture** of Mardi Gras and New Year's Eve.

The game is played **alternately** in Montreal and Toronto. These cities have large stadiums. They also have the best weather for the game. Some people call the Grey Cup "the Arctic ancestor of the Super Bowl."

The Grey Cup was given by Lord Grey. It has become the main **trophy** of Canadian football. At first, the cup was to go to the winner of the amateur football title. Then the cup was changed to a professional award. Some American players have been **imported** to play for Canadian teams.

The rivalry between East and West is **intense.** The Montreal Alouettes won the Grey Cup in 1980, 1984, and 1987. But the Edmonton Eskimos **avenged** the losses in 1988 and 1989. The competition is strong. It continues to make the Grey Cup a matter of national interest in Canada.

MAKE A LIST

>>>> *There are eight vocabulary words in this lesson. In the story, they are boxed in color. Copy the vocabulary words here.*

1. _____debating_____   5. _____trophy_____

2. _____arouses_____   6. _____imported_____

3. _____mixture_____   7. _____intense_____

4. _____alternately_____   8. _____avenged_____

MAKE AN ALPHABETICAL LIST

>>>> *Here are the eight words you copied on the previous page. Write them in alphabetical order in the spaces below.*

mixture	imported	trophy	debating
arouses	alternately	avenged	intense

1. alternately
2. arouses
3. avenged
4. debating
5. imported
6. intense
7. mixture
8. trophy

WHAT DO THE WORDS MEAN?

>>>> *Following are some meanings, or definitions, for the eight vocabulary words in this lesson. Write the words next to their definitions.*

1. trophy — a prize, often a silver cup

2. arouses — stirs up strong feelings; awakens

3. mixture — a combination; something made up by mixing two or more things

4. imported — brought into a country

5. intense — very strong; severe

6. debating — discussing opposing reasons; arguing

7. avenged — took revenge; got even

8. alternately — taking turns; first one and then another

>>>> **Prefixes** are one or more letters attached to the beginning of a word. Prefixes have different meanings. When they join words, they change the meaning of the word. There are many prefixes in our language. A few will be discussed in this lesson. For example:

> **pre** means *"before"*
>
> **pre** + cook = precook (to cook before)

> **super** means *"more than; extra"*
> **super** + human = superhuman (extra special human)

> **un** means *"not; the opposite of"*
>
> **un** + happy = unhappy (not happy)

>>>> *In the following list, connect the prefix with the root word. Write the new word on the lines provided.*

Prefix	Root Word	New Word
un (not; the opposite of)	+ real	= unreal
super (more than; extra)	+ highway	= superhighway
pre (before)	+ paid	= prepaid
dis (not)	+ honest	= dishonest
re (again; back)	+ turn	= return
in (not)	+ complete	= incomplete
sub (under; below)	+ marine	= submarine

>>>> A **synonym** is a word that means the same, or nearly the same, as another word. *Happy* and *glad* are synonyms.

>>>> *The column on the left contains the eight key words in the story. To the right of each key word are three other words or groups of words. Two of these are synonyms for the key word. Circle the two synonyms.*

1. **mixture**   (a combination)   a discovery   (a blend)

2. **imported**   sent out   (brought in)   (taken in)

3. **debating**   (arguing)   (discussing)   ignoring

4. **alternately**   two at a time   (in turns)   (one after the other)

5. **intense**   (very strong)   dull   (sharp)

6. **arouses**   (awakens)   (stirs up)   calms

7. **avenged**   (took revenge)   cheated   (got even)

8. **trophy**   sad event   (winning prize)   (silver cup)

>>>> Two of the words used in the story, *trophy* and *mixture*, are nouns. Think of the trophies and mixtures you have seen or read about. What words can you use to describe them?

>>>> *List as many adjectives as you can that tell something about these nouns. The list has been started for you.*

trophy	mixture
1. silver	1. attractive
2. magnificent	2. interesting
3. Answers will vary.	3. Answers will vary.
4.	4.
5.	5.
6.	6.
7.	7.
8.	8.

>>>> *Look at the picture. What words come into your mind other than the ones you matched with their synonyms? Write them on the lines below. To help you get started, here are two good words:*

1. football

2. game

3. Answers will vary.

4. _____

5. _____

6. _____

7. _____

8. _____

COMPLETE THE STORY

>>>> Here are the eight vocabulary words for this lesson:

trophy	avenged	arouses	imported
debating	intense	alternately	mixture

>>>> *There are four blank spaces in the story below. Four vocabulary words have already been used in the story. They are underlined. Use the other four words to fill in the blanks.*

In the United States, the Super Bowl is a major event. In Canada, the Grey Cup <u>arouses</u> even more excitement. This football game is held ____alternately____ in Toronto and Montreal. These great cities can handle the large crowds. For weeks before the game, much time is spent <u>debating</u> the quality of the teams. No one tries to hide the ____intense____ rivalry between the teams involved.

The Grey Cup has produced outstanding games over the years. Montreal and Edmonton were the rivals in 1977 and 1978. Montreal won the ____trophy____ in 1977; Edmonton <u>avenged</u> the defeat in 1978. In both games, ____imported____ players from American colleges played key roles. This <u>mixture</u> of Canadian and American players gives the game an added interest.

Learn More About Football

>>>> *On a separate piece of paper or in your notebook or journal, complete one or more of the activities below.*

Learning Across the Curriculum

Look at the statistics of a running back of your choice. Figure the average number of *miles* he runs in a year rushing. Or look at the statistics for a quarterback and figure the number of *miles* he has passed in one season. You can find this information in yearly sports almanacs. Ask the librarian if you need some help finding it.

Broadening Your Understanding

Find out more about Canadian football and how it differs from the U.S. version. Make a chart that explains the differences. Then write a paragraph about which game you think would be more exciting and why.

10 THE ROSETTA STONE

Imagine a message so difficult that it took 14 years to **decode!** Think of a **scholar** working day and night to learn the meanings of ancient writings. Jean François Champollion of France worked on a project of this kind for many years. The work was very difficult, but he refused to be **defeated.** The text he studied was carved on a stone found in Rosetta, Egypt. It was named the Rosetta Stone.

The stone was first found by a French **engineer.** He did not think it was important. But then an **archaeologist** found it. There were strange carvings on the stone, called hieroglyphics. These are characters in Egyptian picture writing. Birds with tall crowns, snakes, and **peculiar** figures were carved on the stone.

The **text** was written in three languages. Greek, hieroglyphics, and ancient Egyptian were on the stone. Champollion **translated** the Greek section. Then he compared the Greek words with the hieroglyphics. He also knew the Coptic language. This helped him recognize many Egyptian words. Finally, in 1828, the riddle of the Rosetta Stone was solved. Because of Champollion, scholars today can read hieroglyphics and learn the history of the ancient past.

MAKE A LIST

>>>> *There are eight vocabulary words in this lesson. In the story, they are boxed in color. Copy the vocabulary words here.*

1. decode
2. scholar
3. defeated
4. engineer
5. archaeologist
6. peculiar
7. text
8. translated

MAKE AN ALPHABETICAL LIST

>>>> *Here are the eight words you copied on the previous page. Write them in alphabetical order in the spaces below.*

engineer	scholar	text	translated
peculiar	defeated	decode	archaeologist

1. archaeologist

2. decode

3. defeated

4. engineer

5. peculiar

6. scholar

7. text

8. translated

WHAT DO THE WORDS MEAN?

>>>> *Following are some meanings, or definitions, for the eight vocabulary words in this lesson. Write the words next to their definitions.*

1. text — words and sentences together; a story

2. scholar — a professor; a person of learning

3. defeated — conquered; beaten

4. decode — to solve a puzzle; to find an answer

5. archaeologist — a person who studies ancient life and cultures; a scientist

6. engineer — a person who builds roads and bridges; a specialist in technical fields

7. peculiar — strange; unusual

8. translated — put into words of a different language

76

>>>> **Suffixes** are one or more letters that are attached to the *end* of a word. They also have their own meanings and change the meaning of the new word.

There are many suffixes in our language. We will review the most common ones. Study them carefully. Let's look at some common suffixes and their meanings:

Suffix	Meaning	Word with Suffix	Meaning
ful	full; full of	hand<u>ful</u>	a hand that is full
less	not any; without	home<u>less</u>	without a home
er	a person or thing	teach<u>er</u>	a person who teaches
ish	like	child<u>ish</u>	like a child
ly	in what way	quiet<u>ly</u>	done in a quiet way

>>>> *Here are eight sentences. Read them carefully and add the correct suffix. The suffix should come from the list above.*

1. He ate the pizza slow _____ly_____.
2. That African dance is grace _____ful_____.
3. If you don't study for a test, you're fool _____ish_____.
4. Who, do you think, is a good speak _____er_____.
5. He's liked because he's cheer _____ful_____.
6. She's usual _____ly_____ the first person in line for the bus.
7. Because their work is dangerous, many astronauts are fear _____less_____.
8. I want to be a garden _____er_____.

>>>> A **synonym** is a word that means the same, or nearly the same, as another word. *Happy* and *glad* are synonyms.

>>>> *The column on the left contains the eight key words in the story. To the right of each key word are three other words or groups of words. Two of these are synonyms for the key word. Circle the two synonyms.*

1. **peculiar**   ordinary   (strange)   (odd)

2. **engineer**   (technical director)   weapon carrier   (bridge designer)

3. **decode**   to send a message   (to translate)   (to solve a puzzle)

4. **defeated**   (overcame)   seated   (conquered)

5. **text**   (writings)   (words and sentences)   old papers

6. **scholar**   (professor)   (wise person)   sports announcer

7. **archaeologist**   (one who studies past life)   one who teaches children   (one who studies ancient people)

8. **translated**   guessed   (decoded)   (interpreted)

>>>> There are many words in our language that are often misspelled. These words are spelled incorrectly so many times that they are sometimes called *spelling demons*. (A demon is a devil or an evil spirit—and these words cause a great deal of trouble.) Below there is a correct spelling and an incorrect one.

>>>> *Underline the correct spelling. Then write the word on the line provided. The first one has been done as an example.*

Correct Spelling

1. <u>writing</u>   writting   writing

2. athelete   <u>athlete</u>   athlete

3. <u>government</u>   goverment   government

4. <u>interesting</u>   intresting   interesting

5. <u>across</u>   accross   across

6. cafateria   <u>cafeteria</u>   cafeteria

7. <u>sandwich</u>   sandwitch   sandwich

79

>>>> *Look at the picture. What words come into your mind*
other than the ones you matched with their synonyms?
Write them on the lines below. To help you get started,
here are two good words:

1. _____language_____   5. _____

2. _____writing_____   6. _____

3. ___Answers will vary.___   7. _____

4. _____   8. _____

COMPLETE THE STORY

▶▶▶▶ Here are the eight vocabulary words for this lesson:

engineer	archaeologist	translated	defeated
text	decode	scholar	peculiar

▶▶▶▶ *There are four blank spaces in the story below. Four vocabulary words have already been used in the story. They are underlined. Use the other four words to fill in the blanks.*

The <u>engineer</u> tripped on a large stone. He didn't pay much attention to it. He had more important things to do, like building roads and bridges. So he threw it away. But an _____archaeologist_____ noticed the strange carvings on the stone. These <u>peculiar</u> carvings represented Egyptian picture writing. They were called hieroglyphics. For centuries, this strange picture writing confused scientists. They just couldn't figure out what the pictures meant.

But the _____scholar_____, Jean François Champollion, was determined to work it out. He would _____decode_____ these messages if it took a lifetime. He would not be _____defeated_____. Actually, it was 14 years before he <u>translated</u> the writings. He found the key by comparing three different languages. Once he had solved the riddle, scientists began to work on another <u>text</u>. They could now learn the history of the past.

Learn More About Egypt

▶▶▶▶ *On a separate piece of paper or in your notebook or journal, complete one or more of the activities below.*

Learning Across the Curriculum

The Rosetta Stone has the date 196 B.C. on it. Research what everyday life was like in ancient Egypt. Write about what a day would be like for a person who was living in Egypt then. If you want, draw illustrations to go with your report.

Broadening Your Understanding

Find a book about Egyptian picture writing. Write a note to a friend using this type of writing. Then have your friend write one to you. Then switch notes. Try to read what your friend wrote.

Today Tom Cruise is a big-name movie star. He is recognized everywhere for his skill and **determination.** During the 1980s, he was ranked as one of the top five box-office stars. His performance as a Vietnam veteran in *Born on the Fourth of July* put him on the cover of *Time* magazine. It also earned him an Oscar nomination. Not bad for a boy who went to 11 different schools as he grew up! Cruise remembers **grimly,** "I was always the new kid. Always trying to fight my way to get some **attention** and love."

Cruise had other problems, too. He had a learning **disability.** He found himself in **remedial** classes in each new school. "I could never remember which way the C's and D's went," he says today.

To overcome these challenges, Cruise played sports. He was **frustrated** again and again as his family moved just as he was about to **gain** acceptance.

Finally, at the age of 17, Tom Cruise got a part in a high school production of the musical *Guys and Dolls*. "I just remember feeling so at home on stage, so **relaxed,"** he recalls. It was the beginning of his desire to be an actor. Cruise has also starred in *Risky Business, Top Gun, Rain Man, A Few Good Men,* and *Interview with a Vampire.* He seems completely at home in the movie industry.

MAKE A LIST

>>>> *There are eight vocabulary words in this lesson. In the story, they are boxed in color. Copy the vocabulary words here.*

1. determination
2. grimly
3. attention
4. disability
5. remedial
6. frustrated
7. gain
8. relaxed

MAKE AN ALPHABETICAL LIST

>>>> *Here are the eight words you copied on the previous page. Write them in alphabetical order in the spaces below.*

determination	attention	grimly	frustrated
disability	gain	remedial	relaxed

1. attention
2. determination
3. disability
4. frustrated

5. gain
6. grimly
7. relaxed
8. remedial

WHAT DO THE WORDS MEAN?

>>>> *Following are some meanings, or definitions, for the eight vocabulary words in this lesson. Write the words next to their definitions.*

1. frustrated — discouraged; upset by failure
2. remedial — correcting
3. grimly — harshly
4. determination — firmness of purpose
5. attention — care, notice
6. gain — to get; to earn
7. disability — a disadvantage; an impairment
8. relaxed — calm; at ease

84

>>>> In Lesson 3, you had practice exercises dealing with consonants. Look at the consonants again. In the alphabet, all the letters are consonants except the vowels (*a, e, i, o, u*) and sometimes *y*.

A consonant can be at the beginning of a word, in the middle of a word, or at the end of a word. For example, in the word *cabin,*

> *c* is a beginning consonant
>
> *b* is a medial consonant
>
> *n* is a final consonant

>>>> Here are ten words. See how well you can recognize the beginning, middle, and final consonants.

>>>> *After each word, write the letter* **B** *if the word contains a beginning consonant. Write* **M** *if the word contains a medial consonant. Write* **F** *if the word contains a final consonant.*

Each word on the list contains at least one consonant. Some words contain more than one consonant. The first one has been done for you.

1. read	B, F	**6.** umbrella	M
2. answer	M, F	**7.** writing	B, M, F
3. question	B, M, F	**8.** Olympics	M, F
4. book	B, F	**9.** use	M
5. creep	B, F	**10.** anybody	M

FIND THE SYNONYMS

>>>> A **synonym** is a word that means the same, or nearly the same, as another word. *Happy* and *glad* are synonyms.

>>>> *The column on the left contains the eight key words in the story. To the right of each key word are three other words or groups of words. Two of these are synonyms for the key word. Circle the two synonyms.*

1. **determination** anger (firmness of purpose) (willpower)

2. **grimly** (sadly) cheerfully (seriously)

3. **disability** (injury) (handicap) clumsiness

4. **remedial** stupid (correcting) (curing)

5. **attention** (care) worry (notice)

6. **frustrated** (discouraged) surprised (upset)

7. **gain** (to win) (to earn) to help

8. **relaxed** tense (calm) (comfortable)

>>>> An **adjective** is a word that describes a person, place, or thing. For example, in the sentence "Tom Cruise is a handsome and talented actor," *handsome* and *talented* are adjectives that describe *actor*.

>>>> *Underline the adjectives in the following sentences. The first one has been done as an example.*

1. We had a <u>long</u>, <u>cold</u> wait at the theater to see the <u>famous</u> star.

2. His <u>easy</u> charm makes Tom Cruise a <u>favorite</u> actor.

3. Many of Cruise's <u>younger</u> fans try to copy his <u>cheerful</u>, <u>friendly</u> manner.

4. Even his <u>early</u> pictures show that he would be a <u>special</u> and an <u>exciting</u>, <u>new</u> talent.

5. Behind his <u>good</u> looks, Cruise is a <u>careful</u>, <u>sensitive</u>, and <u>dedicated</u> actor.

USE YOUR OWN WORDS

>>>> *Look at the picture. What words come into your mind other than the ones you matched with their synonyms? Write them on the lines below. To help you get started, here are two good words:*

1. _____ successful _____
2. _____ confident _____
3. _____ Answers will vary. _____
4. _____

5. _____
6. _____
7. _____
8. _____

COMPLETE THE STORY

>>>> Here are the eight vocabulary words for this lesson:

determination	attention	grimly	frustrated
disability	gain	remedial	relaxed

>>>> *There are four blank spaces in the story below. Four vocabulary words have already been used in the story. They are underlined. Use the other four words to fill in the blanks.*

Tom Cruise is someone who has overcome a ___disability___ to reach his goal. His family moved often. He became a ___frustrated___ student when he was unable to fit in at the new schools he attended so often. Other students either ignored him or thought he was not smart because he was in a ___remedial___ reading class. Cruise still remembers how hard it was to get ___attention___ from his classmates.

Cruise worked hard to <u>gain</u> acceptance, but he was never really happy. He still talks <u>grimly</u> about his school days.

In the end, of course, his <u>determination</u> paid off. He took a part in a play and found that he felt completely <u>relaxed</u> on stage. That play was a turning point in his life.

Learn More About The Movies

>>>> *On a separate piece of paper or in your notebook or journal, complete one or more of the activities below.*

Broadening Your Understanding

Watch a movie on T.V. or in a movie theater and write a review of it. Comment on the plot, the characters, the subject, and how well the movie works. Read your movie review to the class.

Extending Your Reading

Special effects are an important part of the movies. Read one of the books below about how moviemakers create realistic characters and scenes. Present your findings to the class.

Movies F/X, by Ian Rimmer
How Movies Are Made, by Gwen Cherrell
Movie Monsters, by Tom Powers

12 A HOME-RUN HITTER

To many people, Edward James Olmos is the picture of **success.** He appeared in the television program "Miami Vice." He has starred in several movies. He won an Academy Award nomination for his role in the movie *Stand and Deliver.*

However, success did not come easy for Olmos. He had to work hard to become a star. Olmos grew up in a poor **area** of Los Angeles. Olmos looked for something to help him get through his rough childhood. He began to play baseball. He worked hard to **improve** his skills. He became the California batting **champion.** He practiced with the major **league** hitters.

Today Olmos says that baseball had a huge **effect** on his life. He learned self-discipline and **patience.** Baseball taught him to be determined and to keep working toward a goal. Olmos used these skills during the years when he was a struggling actor. For a long time, he was only given small parts. He began a furniture delivery business to pay his bills and to **support** his family. He performed at night. In time, Olmos landed bigger parts. He won a Tony Award for his performance in the play *Zoot Suit.* This performance led to more offers. Olmos directed and starred in the movie *American Me.* Olmos reached his goal of stardom. He had hit a home run once again!

MAKE A LIST

>>>> *There are eight vocabulary words in this lesson. In the story, they are boxed in color. Copy the vocabulary words here.*

1. success
2. area
3. improve
4. champion
5. league
6. effect
7. patience
8. support

MAKE AN ALPHABETICAL LIST

>>>> *Here are the eight words you copied on the previous page. Write them in alphabetical order in the spaces below.*

effect	success	area	league
champion	patience	support	improve

1. area
2. champion
3. effect
4. improve

5. league
6. patience
7. success
8. support

WHAT DO THE WORDS MEAN?

>>>> *Following are some meanings, or definitions, for the eight vocabulary words in this lesson. Write the words next to their definitions.*

1. improve — to make better

2. effect — the result; something made to happen; influence

3. league — an association of teams or clubs

4. patience — the willingness to wait; steady effort

5. support — to provide for

6. success — the achievement of something desired

7. champion — the winner of a contest

8. area — a region; a section

>>>> In Lesson 1, you learned the short vowel sounds. In this lesson, you will review the short vowel sounds. Here are some examples of each of the short vowel sounds.

short ă	short ĕ	short ĭ	short ŏ	short ŭ
măp	wĕt	fĭt	mŏp	hŭt

>>>> *Read the following true story and underline the words with short vowel sounds.*

Did you read about Pinky, the circus elephant? He'd turn his head away whenever his master gave him water. He only liked to drink soda. Pinky would put his trunk into the barrel and guzzle up all the soda. He drank so fast that his trunk sucked up a lot of air. Then he'd belch and burp. All the circus people would gather and watch Pinky for their evening fun.

USING YOUR LANGUAGE: Antonyms

>>>> **Antonyms** are words that are opposite in meaning. For example, *good* and *bad* and *fast* and *slow* are antonyms. Here are antonyms for five of the vocabulary words.

>>>> *See if you can find the vocabulary words. Write them in the blank spaces on the left.*

Vocabulary Word	Antonym
1. patience	restlessness
2. success	failure
3. improve	decline
4. champion	loser
5. effect	cause

>>>> A **synonym** is a word that means the same, or nearly the same, as another word. *Happy* and *glad* are synonyms.

>>>> *The column on the left contains the eight key words in the story. To the right of each key word are three other words or groups of words. Two of these are synonyms for the key word. Circle the two synonyms.*

1. **improve**   weaken   (make better)   (increase quality)

2. **area**   (region)   size   (section)

3. **support**   (provide)   abandon   (take care of)

4. **patience**   restlessness   (steady effort)   (endurance)

5. **effect**   cause   (influence)   (result)

6. **league**   sport   (association)   (organization)

7. **champion**   (winner)   (one who comes in first place)   contest

8. **success**   (achievement)   (desired outcome)   loss

USE YOUR OWN WORDS

>>>> *Look at the picture. What words come into your mind other than the ones you matched with their synonyms? Write them on the lines below. To help you get started, here are two good words:*

1. _____actor_____   5. _____
2. ___demonstrating___   6. _____
3. _Answers will vary._   7. _____
4. _____   8. _____

>>>> Here are the eight vocabulary words for this lesson:

success	improve	patience	champion
support	league	area	effect

>>>> *There are four blank spaces in the story below. Four vocabulary words have already been used in the story. They are underlined. Use the other four words to fill in the blanks.*

When Edward James Olmos joined his first baseball _____league_____ he had no idea of the <u>effect</u> the sport would have on his life! He thought the game would simply give him a way of escaping the tough _____area_____ in which he lived. But baseball taught Olmos skills that he would use for the rest of his life. He discovered that through hard work he could <u>improve</u> his skills. He learned to keep focused on his goals. He found that with _____patience_____ and determination, he could become a <u>champion</u>.

Olmos used these same skills to become a famous actor. For years, he worked in small roles. He struggled to _____support_____ his family, often working two jobs. His major break came when he appeared in "Miami Vice." His lead in the picture *Stand and Deliver* marked the greatest point of his journey so far. Edward James Olmos received an Academy Award nomination for the performance. <u>Success</u> was finally his!

>>>> *On a separate piece of paper or in your notebook or journal, complete one or more of the activities below.*

Building Language

Edward James Olmos's lucky break came when he appeared in the play *Zoot Suit*. Use reference texts to find out the meaning of the phrase *zoot suit*. Make a drawing of a zoot suit to share with your class.

Learning Across the Curriculum

Olmos says that baseball had a big influence on his life. Use reference texts to learn more about the origins of this sport. Find out who first created the game, where it was played, and what the original rules were. Share your findings with the class in a short speech.

Broadening Your Understanding

Many television and movie actors are Latinos. Find out about the life of one such actor. Then give a speech to your class while pretending you are that actor. Tell your classmates how you first became involved with acting, the effect it had on your life, and your motto for success.

There was always music in his home. His family sang for fun. They sang while they worked. When not singing, the family listened to classical music. The family's life was *focused* on music. This was the *atmosphere* in which Luciano Pavarotti grew up.

His father was a baker with the soul of a singer. He enjoyed singing at *community* meetings. He hoped his son would one day become a singer. However, Pavarotti wanted to be a professional soccer player.

His mother had *doubts* about her son's plan for the future. She convinced him to become a *primary* school teacher. Even while he taught, Pavarotti studied music and singing. When he won an important *tenor* contest, he left teaching. That same year, he made his debut in the opera *La Bohéme*. Success soon followed. He had the winning mixture of voice and looks. His handsome, *masculine* appearance won many admirers.

Today Pavarotti is considered one of the world's greatest opera stars. Televised broadcasts of his *concerts* have made him quite popular. A 1992 broadcast of his concert with José Carreras and Placido Domingo was viewed by millions of fans. The recording of this concert was the top seller in classical music that year. Through events like this, Pavarotti took classical music out of the opera house and into the living room!

MAKE A LIST

>>>> *There are eight vocabulary words in this lesson. In the story, they are boxed in color. Copy the vocabulary words here.*

1. _____ focused _____

2. _____ atmosphere _____

3. _____ community _____

4. _____ doubts _____

5. _____ primary _____

6. _____ tenor _____

7. _____ masculine _____

8. _____ concerts _____

MAKE AN ALPHABETICAL LIST

>>>> *Here are the eight words you copied on the previous page. Write them in alphabetical order in the spaces below.*

atmosphere	community	tenor	primary
focused	masculine	doubts	concerts

1. atmosphere

2. community

3. concerts

4. doubts

5. focused

6. masculine

7. primary

8. tenor

WHAT DO THE WORDS MEAN?

>>>> *Following are some meanings, or definitions, for the eight vocabulary words in this lesson. Write the words next to their definitions.*

1. tenor — a male singer, often in opera

2. community — people living together in a particular town or district; a group of people

3. masculine — manly; full of strength and vigor

4. focused — concentrated; centered

5. primary — first four years of school; usually refers to kindergarten through grade 3

6. atmosphere — an environment; a mood

7. concerts — musical performances

8. doubts — uncertainties; distrust

100

PHONICS: Reviewing Prefixes

>>>> Remember: **prefixes** are one or more letters attached to the beginning of a root word. Prefixes have different meanings. When they join words they change the meaning of that word. There are many prefixes in our language. Here are a few more to help you figure out word meanings. For example:

auto means "by" or "for" or "of oneself"

co means "with" or "together"

de means "away from" or "off"

mis means "wrong" or "mistake"

fore means "before" or "in front"

inter means "between" or "among"

>>>> *In the following list, connect the prefix with the root word. Write the new word.*

Prefix		Root Word		New Word
1. fore	+	man	=	foreman
2. mis	+	place	=	misplace
3. inter	+	state	=	interstate
4. de	+	frost	=	defrost
5. auto	+	biography	=	autobiography
6. co	+	operate	=	cooperate

>>>> A **synonym** is a word that means the same, or nearly the same, as another word. *Happy* and *glad* are synonyms.

>>>> *The column on the left contains the eight key words in the story. To the right of each key word are three other words or groups of words. Two of these are synonyms for the key word. Circle the two synonyms.*

1. **community**   (group of people)   (town of people)   list of people

2. **masculine**   feminine   (manly)   (of a male)

3. **doubts**   (distrust)   beliefs   (uncertainties)

4. **primary**   (early school years)   grades 9-12   (kindergarten through grade 3)

5. **focused**   (concentrated)   (centered)   wandered

6. **atmosphere**   (environment)   habits   (mood)

7. **tenor**   (singer)   designer   (opera star)

8. **concerts**   books   (musical programs)   (performances)

>>>> **Nouns** are words used to show names of persons, places, things, actions, ideas, and qualities. There are two kinds of nouns, proper and common. **Common nouns** are names of any persons, places, or things, such as *traveler*, *city*, or *box*. **Proper nouns** are names of particular persons, places, or things, such as *Helen*, *New York City*, or *Sears Tower*.

>>>> *Underline the nouns in each of the sentences below. Place one line under each common noun. Place two lines under each proper noun.*

1. Luciano Pavarotti was born in the town of Modena in Italy.

2. His mother convinced him to be a teacher in a primary school.

3. His tour of Australia is one of his fondest memories.

4. Any opera lover can recite the great roles sung by Pavarotti.

5. Pavarotti made his debut in Italian opera as Rodolfo in La Bohème.

6. The singer loved to tell tales of his great performances at the Metropolitan Opera House.

>>>> *Look at the picture. What words come into your mind other than the ones you matched with their synonyms? Write them on the lines below. To help you get started, here are two good words:*

1.   couple   5. _____

2.   hand   6. _____

3.   Answers will vary.   7. _____

4. _____ 8. _____

COMPLETE THE STORY

▶▶▶▶ Here are the eight vocabulary words for this lesson:

focused	doubts	atmosphere	primary
community	masculine	tenor	concerts

▶▶▶▶ *There are four blank spaces in the story below. Four vocabulary words have already been used in the story. They are underlined. Use the other four words to fill in the blanks.*

Pavarotti's early life was <u>focused</u> on music. However, he first became a teacher. He taught in a _____primary_____ school for two years. But he loved the <u>atmosphere</u> of opera. He continued to study music and singing. Then Pavarotti got a big break. He won an important _____tenor_____ contest.

His debut was in the Italian opera *La Bohéme*. After this performance, there were no _____doubts_____ that Pavarotti was destined for stardom. He had just the right combination of voice and _____masculine_____ good looks. He was invited to appear at the world's most famous opera houses. Millions of people viewed his televised <u>concerts</u>. He gained great respect in the special <u>community</u> of opera singers. Many people regard Pavarotti as one of the greatest opera singers ever.

Learn More About Opera

▶▶▶▶ *On a separate piece of paper or in your notebook or journal, complete one or more of the activities below.*

Learning Across the Curriculum

Opera has a long history. Find out something about the history of this art form. Write a short history of the opera. Include why it was first created and who some of the major singers in the history of opera are. Also include information about some of the most famous composers of opera.

Broadening Your Understanding

Arias are the solo songs of opera. Go to the library and listen to some arias. (Mozart and Wagner wrote many arias). Then write a paragraph about these songs. How are the arias you listened to alike? How are they different?

14 SHOOTING BACK

Photographer Jim Hubbard **explores** people's lives through his camera. He wanted to find out more about people who are homeless. He took pictures of some children as they played. One of them was a boy named Dion.

Dion and his family lived in a **hotel** in Washington, DC. Hubbard took pictures of the family. He found that Dion's family was just like other families. Only one thing was different. Dion's family did not have a home.

Dion showed Hubbard some pictures he had taken. Hubbard taught Dion how to take better pictures. Other children asked Hubbard if they could take pictures. Hubbard couldn't help all the kids by himself. He asked other photographers to volunteer their time. The adults gave classes at homeless **shelters.** Many of the children's pictures were **collected.** They were put on **exhibit.** Some photos were used in a book.

The exhibit **resulted** in a **program** called Shooting Back. This program is for homeless children. It helps them express themselves through pictures. It gives them a **sense** of pride. The program also teaches people about the homeless. The pictures show that homeless children are like other children.

MAKE A LIST

>>>> *There are eight vocabulary words in this lesson. In the story, they are boxed in color. Copy the vocabulary words here.*

1. explores
2. hotel
3. shelters
4. collected

5. exhibit
6. resulted
7. program
8. sense

MAKE AN ALPHABETICAL LIST

>>>> *Here are the eight words you copied on the previous page. Write them in alphabetical order in the spaces below.*

collected	shelters	exhibit	program
sense	explores	resulted	hotel

1. collected
2. exhibit
3. explores
4. hotel

5. program
6. resulted
7. sense
8. shelters

WHAT DO THE WORDS MEAN?

>>>> *Following are some meanings, or definitions, for the eight vocabulary words in this lesson. Write the words next to their definitions.*

1. exhibit — to place an object or collection of objects on show

2. hotel — public housing

3. collected — gathered

4. program — organized activities

5. sense — a feeling or impression

6. explores — studies; examines

7. resulted — happened because of something

8. shelters — places that give cover or protection

>>>> In Lesson 4, you learned about beginning digraphs. Now, you're going to learn about digraphs at the *end* of words.

Let's review. **Digraphs** are two consonant sounds that make a single sound. For example:

<u>wh</u> as in <u>wh</u>en (beginning digraph)

<u>sh</u> as in wa<u>sh</u> (final digraph)

<u>ch</u> as in pit<u>ch</u> (final digraph)

Here are some more examples of final digraphs:

ch	sh	gh	ph	th	ck	gn
ea<u>ch</u>	bru<u>sh</u>	cou<u>gh</u>	gra<u>ph</u>	wi<u>th</u>	ba<u>ck</u>	si<u>gn</u>

>>>> *Underline the words in the story below that contain consonant digraphs at the end of words.*

Did you ever <u>wish</u> that you <u>could</u> be an actor? Then you <u>could</u> <u>autograph</u> your <u>photograph</u> and <u>laugh</u> <u>with</u> your fans. You might <u>design</u> a new <u>ranch</u> or a <u>French</u> house. You <u>could</u> <u>watch</u> your own movies or <u>wash</u> your face in a marble <u>bath</u>.

You might choose to play a <u>tough</u> guy. If you practice <u>enough</u>, you should get a chance to sing. Be sure you <u>brush</u> up <u>both</u> skills. If you are picked for a major movie role, you will want to do it right.

FIND THE SYNONYMS

>>>> A **synonym** is a word that means the same, or nearly the same, as another word. *Happy* and *glad* are synonyms.

>>>> *The column on the left contains the eight key words in the story. To the right of each key word are three other words or groups of words. Two of these are synonyms for the key word. Circle the two synonyms.*

1. **explores**   leaves   (searches)   (investigates)

2. **hotel**   public housing   (apartment)   (temporary home)

3. **sense**   (feeling)   hearing   (impression)

4. **exhibit**   (display)   (show)   leave

5. **shelters**   (places that provide protection)   (safe places)   open areas

6. **collected**   spread out   (gathered)   (brought together)

7. **resulted**   (ended)   began   (followed)

8. **program**   (planned events)   directions   (organized system)

>>>> Many times two words are shortened into one by leaving out one or more letters and putting in an apostrophe. The shortened word is called a **contraction.** For example, *I'll* is the contraction for *I will. Don't* is the contraction for *do not.*

>>>> *In the left column are some common contractions. Write the two words the contraction stands for in the right column.*

Contraction	Words Contraction Stands For
1. we'll	we will
2. he'll	he will
3. wouldn't	would not
4. hadn't	had not
5. we're	we are
6. I'm	I am

USE YOUR OWN WORDS

>>>> *Look at the picture. What words come into your mind other than the ones you matched with their synonyms? Write them on the lines below. To help you get started, here are two good words:*

1. ____photography____   5. _____

2. ____homeless____   6. _____

3. __Answers will vary.__   7. _____

4. _____   8. _____

COMPLETE THE STORY

>>>> Here are the eight vocabulary words for this lesson:

exhibit	explores	shelters	hotels
sense	collected	program	resulted

>>>> *There are four blank spaces in the story below. Four vocabulary words have already been used in the story. They are underlined. Use the other four words to fill in the blanks.*

Shooting Back is a _____program_____ designed to help homeless children. Professional photographers volunteer to teach the youngsters how to take photographs. They hold workshops at homeless shelters and sometimes at hotels where poor people are given a room to stay. The adults explain how to use a camera. They teach the children how to take good pictures.

The children are given cameras. They are encouraged to express themselves. Each child explores the world through a camera's lens. The pictures the children take are _____collected_____ and put on _____exhibit_____ .

For the children, the Shooting Back program resulted in a _____sense_____ of pride in what they did. They felt good about themselves and their accomplishments. They also were able to show others what their homeless world is like.

Learn More About Homelessness

>>>> *On a separate piece of paper or in your notebook or journal, complete one or more of the activities below.*

Learning Across the Curriculum

Use reference books to find out the number of homeless people estimated to live in your state. Then determine the homeless population in four other states. Display your findings in a graph.

Broadening Your Understanding

Homelessness is a problem that affects all members of our society. Contact a local homeless shelter in your town. Find out what you can do to help these people. Make a poster that encourages your classmates to help out, too.

15 SAN GENNARO

New York would not be the same without the Festival of San Gennaro. Once a year along Mulberry Street in New York City, there is a feast. The festival is a ten-block *spectacle.* People come to eat, drink, sing, and dance. Everyone is friendly. There are hundreds of booths in the streets. They *overflow* with all kinds of Italian food.

For at least a *generation,* people have honored San Gennaro. He was a third-century bishop. It is said that his prayers saved Naples by stopping a huge volcanic *eruption.*

During the feast, the saint's *bust* is draped in red ribbons. It is carried through the streets of Little Italy, an area in New York City that is primarily Italian. A service is held in honor of the saint. Then the statue is taken to a shrine where it has the place of honor.

The feast lasts 11 days. Every night is *exciting.* There are many arches aglow with the light of 2 million bulbs. Musicians play love songs. The air is filled with *romance.* After watching street dances, people eat and enjoy themselves until they are *weary.* Everyone is welcome at the San Gennaro Festival. Perhaps you can join the fun someday.

MAKE A LIST

>>>> *There are eight vocabulary words in this lesson. In the story, they are boxed in color. Copy the vocabulary words here.*

1. _spectacle_
2. _overflow_
3. _generation_
4. _eruption_
5. _bust_
6. _exciting_
7. _romance_
8. _weary_

MAKE AN ALPHABETICAL LIST

>>>> *Here are the eight words you copied on the previous page. Write them in alphabetical order in the spaces below.*

romance	overflow	spectacle	bust
weary	eruption	exciting	generation

1. _____bust_____

2. _____eruption_____

3. _____exciting_____

4. _____generation_____

5. _____overflow_____

6. _____romance_____

7. _____spectacle_____

8. _____weary_____

WHAT DO THE WORDS MEAN?

>>>> *Following are some meanings, or definitions, for the eight vocabulary words in this lesson. Write the words next to their definitions.*

1. _____eruption_____ the bursting forth of a volcano; throwing out of lava

2. _____weary_____ tired; worn out

3. _____exciting_____ stirring; thrilling

4. _____generation_____ a period of time (approximately 30 years); people living during the same period of time

5. _____spectacle_____ an unusual sight; an elaborate show or display

6. _____overflow_____ to flow or spread over

7. _____bust_____ a piece of sculpture representing the upper part of the body; a statue

8. _____romance_____ a feeling of love and adventure; affection

116

>>>> In Lesson 6, you were introduced to consonant blends. Remember: **Consonant blends** are made by two or three consonants coming together. They can appear at the beginning, middle, and end of words. In Lesson 6, you worked with beginning blends. Now you will work with blends at the *end* of words. For example:

st	sk	ng	nd	nk	lf
fea<u>st</u>	de<u>sk</u>	ba<u>ng</u>	sa<u>nd</u>	tha<u>nk</u>	se<u>lf</u>
wri<u>st</u>	fla<u>sk</u>	ra<u>ng</u>	e<u>nd</u>	ba<u>nk</u>	she<u>lf</u>

>>>> *Complete the following sentences by supplying a word that ends with a consonant blend. Use only those words that appear in the examples above. The first one has been done as an example.*

1. A synonym for *loud noise* is _____bang_____.

2. For the many favors you have done, I say "_____thank_____ you."

3. The small part of your arm above your hand is called your _____wrist_____.

4. The reference books can be found on the top _____shelf_____.

5. We had so many good things to eat that our meal could be called a _____feast_____.

6. Don't keep too much cash on hand. It is always better to deposit it in a _____bank_____.

7. If I don't straighten the top of my _____desk_____, I'll never find my homework.

8. I can't wait until I reach the _____end_____ of my book.

>>>> A **synonym** is a word that means the same, or nearly the same, as another word. *Happy* and *glad* are synonyms.

>>>> *The column on the left contains the eight key words in the story. To the right of each key word are three other words or groups of words. Two of these are synonyms for the key word. Circle the two synonyms.*

1. **spectacle**   a spy   (a display)   (a great show)

2. **romance**   (love)   (affection)   foolishness

3. **overflow**   (to run over)   (to spread over)   to see over

4. **eruption**   (throwing out)   slowing down   (bursting forth)

5. **exciting**   (stirring)   puzzling   (thrilling)

6. **generation**   a forgotten time   (a period of time)   (people living in the same time period)

7. **weary**   (fatigued)   overjoyed   (tired)

8. **bust**   (a sculpture of the upper part of the body)   (a statue)   a shelf

>>>> *In each of the following sentences, there are words that require capital letters. Rewrite each sentence so the words are correctly capitalized. Remember that capital letters are used in the following places: first word in a sentence; names of people, cars, cities, states, countries, holidays, days of the week, and months of the year.*

1. naples was saved by saint gennaro, who stopped the eruption of mount vesuvius.

   Naples was saved by Saint Gennaro, who stopped the eruption of

   Mount Vesuvius.

2. every september along mulberry street in new york city, there is a festival that honors san gennaro.

   Every September along Mulberry Street in New York City, there is a

   festival that honors San Gennaro.

3. if you enjoy italian food from rome and genoa, hurry to the booth at the corner of mulberry street and second avenue.

   If you enjoy Italian food from Rome and Genoa, hurry to the booth at

   the corner of Mulberry Street and Second Avenue.

>>>> **Look at the picture. What words come into your mind other than the ones you matched with their synonyms? Write them on the lines below. To help you get started, here are two good words:**

1. ___grill___

2. ___food___

3. ___Answers will vary.___

4. _____

5. _____

6. _____

7. _____

8. _____

COMPLETE THE STORY

>>>> Here are the eight vocabulary words for this lesson:

overflow	eruption	bust	generation
weary	exciting	romance	spectacle

>>>> *There are four blank spaces in the story below. Four vocabulary words have already been used in the story. They are underlined. Use the other four words to fill in the blanks.*

You are on your way to the San Gennaro Festival. All year, you have waited for this _____exciting_____ <u>spectacle</u>. Ahead of you is an evening of fun and food. You haven't eaten all day. You know the booths will _____overflow_____ with all kinds of food. Here's your chance to sample dozens of tasty items. Just don't overdo it.

The colorful parade begins. Hundreds of people crowd around the <u>bust</u> of Saint Gennaro. They rush to pin dollar bills on the red ribbons. Not many people know that Saint Gennaro saved Naples by stopping the _____eruption_____ of a great volcano.

Late that night, you return home. You are _____weary_____ from hours of dancing and singing. But everything was so cheerful and lovely. It was a night of <u>romance</u>. You are pleased that this festival is part of your <u>generation</u>. You hope that it will continue for many more years.

Learn More About Festivals

>>>> *On a separate piece of paper or in your notebook or journal, complete one or more of the activities below.*

Appreciating Diversity

Find out about a festival in your native country. Imagine you are walking through the festival. Write about what you think it is like to be there. What do you see? What do you hear? What do you smell?

Broadening Your Understanding

People plan festivals for everything from strawberries to saints. Go to the library and look in travel books for a book about an area you would like to visit. Then find out what festivals you might see there. Write about the festival you would most like to see.

A

accept *[AK sept]* to agree to take or receive

achieve *[uh CHEEV]* to reach a desired goal

acrobat *[AK ruh bat]* a skilled gymnast; an expert in tumbling

admitted *[ad MIT ted]* gave permission to enroll as a student; allowed to enter

aerialist *[AIR ee uh list]* a person who performs on a trapeze

afford *[uh FOHRD]* to have the ability to purchase something

agile *[AJ ul]* having quick, easy movements; limber

aid *[AYD]* to help; to give what is useful or necessary

alert *[uh LURT]* quick in thought and action; watchful

alternately *[AWL tur nit lee]* taking turns; first one and then another

appeared *[uh PEERD]* was seen (on stage or screen); performed

archaeologist *[ar kee OL uh jist]* a person who studies ancient life and cultures; a scientist

area *[AYR ee uh]* a region; a section

arouses *[uh ROUZ ez]* stirs up strong feelings; awakens

ashamed *[uh SHAYMD]* embarrassed; feeling shame

atmosphere *[AT mus feer]* an environment; a mood

attention *[uh TEN shun]* notice, care

avenged *[uh VENJD]* took revenge; got even

B

background *[BAK ground]* accompanying the main action

bouquets *[boo KAYZ]* bunches of flowers fastened together

bust *[BUST]* a piece of sculpture representing the upper part of the body; a statue

C

capital *[KAP uh tul]* the city where government meets

champion *[CHAM pee ohn]* the winner of a contest

collapsed *[kul LAPSD]* broke down suddenly; fell down

collected *[kuh LEKT uhd]* gathered

combines *[kum BYNZ]* joins together; mixes

community *[kuh MYOO nih tee]* people living together in a particular town or district; a group of people

composer *[kom POH zur]* a person who writes music

concerts *[KOHN suhrtz]* musical performances

construction *[kun STRUK shun]* the process of building

D

debating *[dih BAYT ing]* discussing opposing reasons; arguing

decode *[dee KOHD]* to solve a puzzle; to find an answer

defeated *[dih FEET id]* conquered; beaten

descents *[dee SENTS]* downward passages

detect *[dih TEKT]* to discover; to find out

determination *[dih TUR muh NAY shun]* firmness of purpose

disability *[dis uh BIL uh tee]* a disadvantage; an impairment

doubts *[DOWTS]* uncertainties; distrust

E

ease *[EEZ]* a natural way or manner

ecstatic *[ek STAT ik]* very happy or joyful

effect *[e FEKT]* the result; something made to happen; influence

engineer *[en juh NEER]* a person who builds roads and bridges; a specialist in technical fields

eruption *[ih RUP shun]* bursting forth of a volcano; throwing out of lava

example *[eg ZAM pul]* a model

exciting *[ek SY ting]* stirring; thrilling

exhibit *[eks IB it]* to place an object or collection of objects on show

expensive *[ek SPENS iv]* costly; high-priced

experience *[ek SPIHR ee uhns]* the act of living through an event

explores *[ek SPLOHRZ]* studies or examines

F

focused *[FOH kusd]* concentrated; centered

foreman *[FOR man]* a person in charge of a group of workers; a boss

fraction *[FRAK shun]* a small part; less than a second in time

frustrated *[FRUS trayt id]* discouraged; upset by failure

G

gain *[GAYN]* to get; to earn

generation *[jen uh RAY shun]* a period of time (approximately 30 years); people living during the same period of time

grand [GRAND] large; important; complete

grimly *[GRIM lee]* harshly

H

hailed *[HAYLD]* praised; saluted

harvesting *[HAHR vihs ting]* gathering of crops

hotel *[hoh TEL]* public housing

I

imported *[im PORT id]* brought into a country

improve *[im PROOV]* to make better

incredible *[in KRED uh bul]* almost impossible to believe

inquiries *[IN kwuh reez]* questions

intense *[in TENS]* very strong; severe

intrigued *[in TREEGD]* interested; aroused by curiosity

J

jacket *[JAK it]* a short coat

justice *[JUS tis]* fairness; rightfulness

L

league *[LEEG]* an association of teams or clubs

legal *[LEE gul]* having to do with the law or with lawyers

limits *[LIM its]* borders; stopping places

M

major *[MAY jor]* main; principal

masculine *[MAS kyoo lin]* manly; full of strength and vigor

mixture *[MIKS chur]* a combination; something made up by mixing two or more things

O

objected *[ob JECT id]* spoke out against; protested

opponents *[uh POH nents]* enemies; those who disagree

outfit *[OUT fit]* a group; a team

overflow *[oh vur FLOW]* to flow or spread over

P

patience *[PAY shuhns]* the willingness to wait; steady effort

peculiar *[pih KYOOL yur]* strange; unusual

plentiful [PLEN tih ful] more than enough; abundant
primary [PRY mayr ree] first four years of school; usually refers to kindergarten through grade 3
program [PROH gram] organized activities

R

rebel [REB ul] a person who goes against the system; one who resists authority
rejected [rih JEKT id] refused or turned away
relaxed [rih LAKSD] calm; at ease
remedial [rih MEE dee ul] correcting
reminded [rih MYND uhd] thought of something again
remote [rih MOHT] faraway; unsettled
resolved [rih ZOLVD] determined; fixed in purpose
responds [rih SPONDZ] answers; replies
resulted [rih ZULT uhd] happened because of something
romance [roh MANS] a feeling of love and adventure; affection
rotation [roh TAY shun] taking turns in a regular order; one following the other

S

scenery [SEE nuh ree] painted pictures or hangings for a stage
scholar [SKOL ur] a professor; a person of learning
sense [SENTZ] a feeling or impression
shelters [SHEL tuhrz] places that give cover or protection
singular [SING gyoo lur] worthy of notice; remarkable
skill [SKIL] the ability to use one's knowledge in doing something
somersaults [SUM ur sawlts] acrobatic stunts; full body turns, forward or backward

spectacle [SPEK tuh kul] an unusual sight; an elaborate show or display
stunt [STUNT] a daring trick; a display of skill
substances [SUB stan ses] materials from which something is made
success [suhk SES] the achievement of something desired
support [suh POHRT] to provide for

T

talents [TAL unts] special or natural abilities; skills
tenor [TEN ur] male singer, often in opera
terrain [tuh RAYN] the ground
text [TEKST] words and sentences together; a story
translated [trans LAYT id] put into words of a different language
trapeze [tra PEEZ] a short horizontal bar, hung by two ropes, on which aerialists perform
trophy [TROH fee] a prize, often a silver cup
tuck [TUK] to pull in; to draw in closely

U

undergo [un der GOH] to experience; to go through
upset [up SET] distressed; disturbed

V

venturesome [VEN chur sum] seeking adventure; daring; bold
visibility [viz uh BIL uh tee] ability to see

W

weary [WEER ee] tired; worn out
widows [WID ohz] women whose husbands have died